THE GREAT BOOK OF
NASCAR LISTS

THE GREAT BOOK OF NASCAR LISTS

by John Roberts with MB Roberts
foreword by Kyle Petty

RUNNING PRESS
PHILADELPHIA · LONDON

© 2012 by John Roberts
Published by Running Press,
A Member of the Perseus Books Group

All rights reserved under the Pan-American and International
Copyright Conventions
Printed in the United States

Books published by Running Press are available at special discounts for bulk pur-
chases in the United States by corporations, institutions, and other organizations.
For more information, please contact the Special Markets Department at the
Perseus Books Group, 2300 Chestnut Street, Suite 200, Philadelphia, PA 19103, or
call (800) 810-4145, ext. 5000, or e-mail special.markets@perseusbooks.com.

ISBN 978-0-7624-4296-6
Library of Congress Control Number: 2011941635

E-book ISBN 978-0-7624-4638-4

9 8 7 6 5 4 3 2 1
Digit on the right indicates the number of this printing

Cover design by Matthew Goodman
Interior design by Josh McDonald
Edited by Geoffrey Stone
Typography: Helvetica, and Boton

Running Press Book Publishers
2300 Chestnut Street
Philadelphia, PA 19103-4371

Visit us on the web!
www.runningpress.com

Contents

Introduction

There's always that guy. The one in every crowd who says, "NASCAR isn't a sport." And you know, he just may be right. The sport is what happens on the race track. But NASCAR is more than a sport; it's a way of life. People involved in the stick-and-ball sports might practice for a couple hours a day, for about six months out of the year. Most people involved in preparing race cars for competition work seven days a week, from 7:00 a.m. to 7:00 p.m., for most of the year.

Fans of other sports tailgate for two hours; NASCAR fans tailgate for two or three days. And NASCAR is the only place that a blue tarp thrown over a pickup truck creates a camper. It's all about passion. These competitors are passionate about their craft, and the fans are passionate about this sport.

With that in mind, we present to you the best of NASCAR in a series of lists that we hope fuels your passion for the greatest form of motorsports competition in the world.

This is a fun book. NASCAR is and always will be basically about fun. Fans have fun going to the races, drivers have fun competing, and the people who build the cars and get them to the track do it because it's fun.

We broadcasters definitely have a lot of fun talking about racing. And putting these lists together was a great way to pass the time in between races. Thanks to everybody who pitched in. Who needs Google when you've got walking, talking NASCAR encyclopedias hanging around the track?

Enjoy!

John Roberts

Foreword

No matter what the topic is, when it comes to naming the best of all time, "the best" is always arguable. In NASCAR, there was a best in the beginning, the best in the 1960s, the best in the 1970s and '80s, and there's the best now.

It's almost like rock music. When you're talking about the best, you're talking about the best of a certain period. I don't think you can compare the Beatles and the Rolling Stones to Nirvana or anybody else. It's always subjective.

When it comes to making a list of the best or the worst or the most in NASCAR, besides considering the era of the driver, many other things come into play. Mostly, the opinion of the list-maker.

A guy can look at a list and see that Dale Earnhardt Sr. is number one, but somebody is always going to put Richard Petty above him or somebody else is always going to put Dale Jr. above another guy. Regardless of who won or who led the most laps.

Race fans love trivia. But most of them don't let the facts get in the way. Even when they know the facts, or especially when they are pretending to know the facts. NASCAR fans let their hearts tell them what their lists should be.

Kyle Petty

To celebrate its fiftieth anniversary in 1998, NASCAR called upon an independent panel of experts—consisting of drivers, team owners, crew chiefs, media members, track operators, and others closely associated with racing—to compile a list of NASCAR's 50 greatest drivers. No easy task. The full list of 50 appears below in alphabetical order. Quibble if you must about who is and who isn't on it. But this here is a great list.

The living members of this group of all-time greats were honored on February 15, 1998, during a prerace ceremony prior to the Daytona 500. Since then, several members of this group have been inducted into the NASCAR Hall of Fame, which opened in 2010.

(Note: drivers with an asterisk after their names are NASCAR Hall of Fame Inductees.)

50. Bobby Allison*

49. Davey Allison

48. Buck Baker

47. Buddy Baker

46. Geoffrey Bodine

45. Neil Bonnett

44. Red Byron

43. Jerry Cook

42. Dale Earnhardt Sr.*

41. Ralph Earnhardt

40. Bill Elliott

39. Richie Evans*

38. Red Farmer

37. Tim Flock

36. A. J. Foyt

35. Harry Gant

34. Jeff Gordon

33. Ray Hendrick

32. Jack Ingram

31. Ernie Irvan

30. Bobby Isaac

29. Dale Jarrett

28. Ned Jarrett*

27. Junior Johnson*

26. Alan Kulwicki

25. Terry Labonte

24. Fred Lorenzen

23. Tiny Lund

22. Mark Martin

21. Hershel McGriff

20. Cotton Owens

19. Marvin Panch

18. Benny Parsons

17. David Pearson*

16. Lee Petty*

15. Richard Petty*

14. Tim Richmond

13. Fireball Roberts

12. Ricky Rudd

11. Marshall Teague

10. Herb Thomas

9. Curtis Turner

8. Rusty Wallace

7. Darrell Waltrip*

6. Joe Weatherly

5. Bob Welborn

4. Rex White

3. Glen Wood*

2. Cale Yarborough*

1. LeeRoy Yarbrough

Before a race in 2006, then 51-year-old driver Ken Schrader told a reporter, "The car doesn't know how old you are or how much you weigh." Several years later, at age 56 and counting, Schrader is still competing on the race track, although he doesn't disclose his weight.

Certainly, experience matters and some drivers continue to drive and win despite the ticking clock. But do things really get better with age?

Back in the early 1990s, Harry Gant won eight NASCAR Sprint Cup Series races after turning 50, and his last Coors Light Pole Award was at Bristol Motor Speedway in 1994, when he was 54 years old. More recently, Mark Martin has won five races (and counting) after turning 50.

Then there's James Hylton. By qualifying for the NASCAR Nationwide Series race at Darlington Raceway at age 76 in 2011, Hylton, who began racing in 1964, became the oldest driver to make the field in one of NASCAR's top three series. By doing so, Hylton broke his own mark, set three years prior when he qualified for the NASCAR Nationwide Series race in Daytona at age 73.

Hylton isn't just a novelty, either. He is an active ARCA competitor who finished 19th in driver points in 2010. And he's not the only septuagenarian in NASCAR history. In 1998, Bobby Myers became the oldest NASCAR Camping World Truck Series driver when he competed at Homestead at age 70.

So here's a nod to those who think in terms of taking tires rather than retiring. And there's absolutely no truth to the rumor that these guys leave their right-turn signal on for the duration of the race.

5. Dick Trickle (age 60). Dover International Speedway, June 2, 2002.

4. Dave Marcis (age 61). Daytona International Speedway, February 17, 2002.

3. Morgan Shepherd (age 64). New Hampshire Motor Speedway, September 17, 2006.

2. Jim Fitzgerald (age 65). Riverside International Raceway, June 21, 1987.

1. Hershel McGriff (age 65). Infineon Raceway, May 16, 1993.

Driver Nicknames

Drivers, pit crew guys, and race team owners love to give each other nicknames. The catchy ones tend to stick, which is sometimes a good thing and sometimes a bad thing for the nickname-ee.

Most likely, Kurt "Ears" Busch didn't love being reminded of his oversized ears on a daily basis. His younger brother, Kyle, must have been glad to graduate from "Shrub" to his newer and much preferred nickname, "Rowdy." And it's just a guess, but Tony Stewart probably prefers "Smoke" to some of his other nicknames.

Here are a few monikers (listed alphabetically) that stuck to drivers, for better or for worse.

29. "The Gentle Giant" or "Crisco Kid" — Buddy Baker

28. "Red" — Robert Byron

27. "The Intimidator" or "The Man in Black" — Dale Earnhardt Sr.

26. "Ironheart" — Ralph Earnhardt

25. "June Bug" or "Little E" — Dale Earnhardt Jr.

24. "Cousin Carl" — Carl Edwards

23. "Awesome Bill from Dawsonville" or "Million Dollar Bill" — Bill Elliott

22. "Handsome Harry Gant" — Harry Gant

21. "Happy" — Kevin Harvick

20. "Swervin' Irvan" — Ernie Irvan

19. "Gentleman Ned" — Ned Jarrett

18. "The Polish Prince" or "Special K" — Alan Kulwicki

17. **"The Ironman"** — Terry Labonte

16. **"Sliced Bread"** — Joey Logano

15. **"Tiny"** — DeWayne Lund

14. **"Coo Coo"** — Clifton Marlin

13. **"The King"** — Richard Petty

12. **"The Silver Fox"** — David Pearson

11. **"Fireball"** — Glenn Roberts

10. **"Shorty"** — Lloyd Rollins

9. **"Iron Man"** — Ricky Rudd

8. **"Mr. Excitement"** — Jimmy Spencer

7. **"Speedy"** — Alfred Thompson

6. **"Herman the German"** — Kenny Wallace

5. **"Rubberhead"** — Rusty Wallace

4. **"Jaws"** — Darrell Waltrip

3. **"The Clown Prince of NASCAR"** — Joe Weatherly

2. **"Woodchopper"** — Glen Wood

1. **"The Timmonsville Flash"** — Cale Yarborough

And you, too, crew guys and team owners.

6. Robert Barker, crew chief for Casey Mears and others: "Bootie"

5. Danny Myers, Dale Earnhardt Sr.'s longtime gas man: "Chocolate"

4. Mike McSwain, crew chief for Ricky Rudd, Bobby Labonte, and others: "Fatback"

3. Jeff Gordon's crew: The Rainbow Warriors

2. Henry Yunick, 1950s and 1960s crew chief and car owner: "Smokey"

1. Jack Roush, founder and CEO of the Roush Fenway Racing team: "Cat in the Hat"

Over the years, most every NASCAR race track has earned its own nickname. Here are a few favorites.

13. "Thunder Valley" or "The World's Fastest Half-Mile" – Bristol Motor Speedway

12. "Beast of the Southeast" – Charlotte Motor Speedway

11. The "Track Too Tough to Tame" or "The Lady in Black" – Darlington Raceway

10. "World Center of Racing" – Daytona International Speedway

9. "The Monster Mile" or "White Lightning" – Dover International Speedway

8. "The Brickyard" – Indianapolis Motor Speedway

7. "Diamond in the Desert" – Las Vegas Motor Speedway

6. "The Paperclip" – Martinsville Speedway

5. "The Magic Mile" – New Hampshire Motor Speedway

4. "The Bermuda Triangle" – Pocono Raceway

3. "The Glen" – Watkins Glen International

2. "The Great American Speedway" – Texas Motor Speedway

1. "The Rock" – Rockingham Speedway

Most Popular Drivers

More than any other sports celebrities, NASCAR drivers are known to be approachable and down-to-earth folks. For the most part, they are all really nice people.

Fans know which drivers they like best and show their love by voting annually for the NASCAR NMPA Most Popular Driver Award, a prize that has been given out by the National Motorsports Press Association every year since 1956. Bill Elliott has won it the most times (16), followed by Richard Petty (10). Dale Jr. is currently on a roll with eight in a row and counting.

Here are all the past winners of this award, each of them guys that couldn't be faulted for saying, "You like me. You really like me."

25. Dale Earnhardt Jr. (2003–2010)

24. Bill Elliott (2002)

23. Dale Earnhardt Sr. (2001)

22. Bill Elliott (1991–2000)

21. Darrell Waltrip (1989–1990)

20. Bill Elliott (1984–1988)

19. Bobby Allison (1981–1983)

18. David Pearson (1979–1980)

17. Richard Petty (1974–1978)

16. Bobby Allison (1971–1973)

15. **Richard Petty (1970)**

14. **Bobby Isaac (1969)**

13. **Richard Petty (1968)**

12. **Cale Yarborough (1967)**

11. **Darel Dieringer (1966)**

10. **Fred Lorenzen (1965)**

9. **Richard Petty (1964)**

8. **Fred Lorenzen (1963)**

7. **Richard Petty (1962)**

6. **Joe Weatherly (1961)**

5. **Rex White (1960)**

4. **Junior Johnson (1959)**

3. **Glen Wood (1958)**

2. **Fireball Roberts (1957)**

1. **Curtis Turner (1956)**

The 10 Oldest Drivers to Win a NASCAR Sprint Cup Series Race

"I'm so old they've discontinued my blood type." – Dick Trickle

It's one thing to start a race. And another to finish it—especially in first place. Here are the 10 oldest drivers to win NASCAR Sprint Cup Series races, along with where and when they won them.

10. Richard Petty (47 years, 2 days). Daytona International Speedway, July 4, 1984.

9. Geoffrey Bodine (47 years, 3 months, 24 days). Watkins Glen International, August 11, 1996.

8. Rusty Wallace (47 years, 8 months, 4 days). Martinsville Speedway, April 18, 2004.

7. Bill Elliott (48 years, 1 month, 1 day). Rockingham Speedway, November 9, 2003.

6. Dale Jarrett (48 years, 10 months, 6 days). Talladega Superspeedway, October 2, 2005.

5. Dale Earnhardt Sr. (49 years, 5 months, 16 days). Talladega Superspeedway, October 15, 2000.

4. Bobby Allison (50 years, 2 months, 11 days). Daytona International Speedway, February 14, 1988.

3. Mark Martin (50 years, 8 months, 11 days). New Hampshire Motor Speedway, September 20, 2009.

2. Morgan Shepherd (51 years, 5 months, 8 days). Atlanta Motor Speedway, March 20, 1993.

1. Harry Gant (52 years, 7 months, 6 days). Michigan International Speedway, August 6, 1992.

It wasn't that long ago that rookies didn't get into top cars. Period. They started out with lower-tier teams and slowly worked their way up from there. Dale Jarrett once said it took him 12 years to become an overnight sensation. But now, when a rookie bursts onto the NASCAR Sprint Cup Series scene, he is given the opportunity to win, and, generally, they are expected to win. Jimmie Johnson was actually a legitimate championship contender in his rookie year of 2002. Since 1979, six Rookie of the Year winners have later won a NASCAR Sprint Cup Series championship—Dale Earnhardt (1979), Rusty Wallace (1984), Alan Kulwicki (1986), Jeff Gordon (1993), Tony Stewart (1999), and Matt Kenseth (2000).

Here are some of the top rookies—all NASCAR Sprint Cup Series Rookie of the Year (ROTY) winners—who took the NASCAR world by storm from the start.

13. Joey Logano (2009). The third Joe Gibbs Racing driver to win ROTY (following Tony Stewart in 1999 and Denny Hamlin in 2006), Logano also set the mark as the youngest driver (age 19) to win the award.

12. Regan Smith (2008). The first Rookie of the Year in the 52-year history of the program to finish every race he started (in his case, 34), Smith edged out fellow rookie Sam Hornish Jr. for the ROTY award by only seven points.

11. Dale Earnhardt Sr. (1979). Despite tough competition from fellow newcomers Joe Millikan, Harry Gant, and Terry Labonte, Earnhardt took Rookie of the Year honors even after a four-week layoff. The following year, he was NASCAR Sprint Cup champion.

10. Kasey Kahne (2004). Kasey Kahne blasted onto the scene his first year. In just his second NASCAR Sprint Cup race, he finished runner-up to 2003 NASCAR Sprint Cup champion Matt Kenseth, who beat him by a mere 0.01 seconds. In his third race, he again finished just behind Kenseth, this time by 3.4 seconds. At season's end, the 24-year-old Kahne became the youngest NASCAR Sprint Cup Rookie of the Year since Jeff Gordon in 1993.

9. Jeff Gordon (1993). No one was surprised when 22-year-old Jeff Gordon won NASCAR Sprint Cup Rookie of the Year in 1993. He'd been winning short-track races since age five, and the first year he made the switch from open-wheel racing to NASCAR, he was named 1991 NASCAR Nationwide Series Rookie of the Year. During his debut NASCAR season, he posted seven top five and 11 top 10 finishes in 30 races.

8. Davey Allison (1987). Despite starting just 22 of 29 NASCAR Sprint Cup races during his rookie season of 1987, Allison tallied eight front-row starts, including a record five Coors Light Pole Awards and two wins (at Talledega and Dover) on his way to becoming ROTY.

7. Denny Hamlin (2006). In 2006, Hamlin stacked up two wins (sweeping at Pocono), eight top five and 20 top 10 finishes on his way to being named NASCAR Sprint Cup Rookie of the Year. He also qualified for the Chase and finished third in the final points standings, a record for a rookie at the time.

6. Ryan Newman (2002). As a rookie in 2002, Newman won one NASCAR Sprint Cup race (at New Hampshire) and nudged out another promising newcomer, Jimmie Johnson (the first rookie in history to lead the points standings), for ROTY honors after earning a record six Coors Light Pole Awards and finishing in the top five 14 times and in the top 10 a total of 22 times.

5. Kevin Harvick (2001). After the 2001 Daytona 500, car owner Richard Childress asked NASCAR Nationwide Series driver Kevin Harvick to take Dale Earnhardt Sr.'s place for the rest of the season. Harvick accepted the honor and became the first driver to go full time in both the NASCAR Nationwide Series and NASCAR Sprint Cup Series. He also became the first driver to win a NASCAR Nationwide Series championship and NASCAR Sprint Cup Series Rookie of the Year in the same season.

4. Jamie McMurray (2003). After driving for injured teammate Sterling Marlin in 2002, McMurray made his official NASCAR Sprint Cup debut the following year, winning in just his second race. After a few bobbles that season, McMurray found his stride, placing in the top 10 in half of his last 16 races, finishing 13th overall and snagging ROTY honors.

3. Ron Bouchard (1981). At age 32, Bouchard was an unlikely rookie. He also did some very unlikely things on the track, such as win a NASCAR Sprint Cup race during his first season. That just wasn't done back then. From the start of the modern era in 1972 through 1998, only five drivers won a NASCAR Sprint Cup race as a rookie—Earl Ross (1974), Dale Earnhardt Sr. (1979), Morgan Shepherd (1981), Bouchard (1981), and Davey Allison (1987). Even though he never won another NASCAR Sprint Cup race during his career, Bouchard's rookie run, during which he notched five top five finishes and one Coors Light Pole Award, was something to remember.

2. Matt Kenseth (2000). After making his way through the ranks, newcomer Matt Kenseth hit the NASCAR Nationwide Series in 1997 and placed second in Rookie of the Year points. In 2000, he was named NASCAR Sprint Cup Series Rookie of the Year, a prelude to his championship just three years later.

1. Tony Stewart (1999). It's a big deal for a rookie to win one race. Stewart won three in 1999 and finished the season ranked fourth overall with 12 top five finishes, 21 top 10 finishes, and a remarkable run of 15 top 10 finishes in a 19-week span. This ROTY also drove in the Indy 500 the same day he competed in the Coca-Cola 600, finishing fourth and ninth respectively.

Several female drivers and executives have indisputably made their mark over the years. And the girls are watching the races, too. Women comprise about 40 percent of NASCAR's fan base. Who knows how many future NASCAR stars are among them?

Honorable Mention. Linda Vaughn. Women in NASCAR are so much more than trophy girls and beauty queens. Still, it would be an oversight not to give the queen of the queens her due. Linda Vaughn, who began her race track "career" in 1961 when she was named Miss Atlanta Raceway, was a familiar and welcome sight at dozens of races during the 1960s, '70s, and early '80s. From her title as Miss Pure Firebird to her best-known reign (as Miss Hurst Golden Shifter), Vaughn was a classic.

14. Erin Crocker. In 2005, Crocker made her NASCAR debut at Richmond International Raceway, where she drove the No. 6 Country Crock Spread Dodge for Evernham Motorsports. In 2006, Crocker was the only woman to compete full time in the NASCAR Camping World Truck Series.

13. Carolyn Carrier. One of NASCAR's most successful promoters got her start selling tickets at her father's track, Bristol International Speedway (now Bristol Motor Speedway), when it opened in 1960. She went on to work for H.A. "Humpy" Wheeler at Charlotte Motor Speedway and Mike Helton at Talladega Superspeedway. Then, after handling marketing and public relations for Bobby Allison Motorsports for five years, she opened her own agency, THAT'S RACIN'! Inc., in 1996, where her past and present list of clients include Brett Bodine's NASCAR Sprint Cup Series team, the Official Directory of NASCAR, the Ertl Company, and Stock Car Racing magazine.

12. Jody Deery. When her husband, Hugh Deery, passed away in 1984, Jody Deery took over management of the Rockford Speedway, a nationally acclaimed NASCAR Whelen All-American Series quarter-mile oval. Over the years, the matriarch of one of short-track racing's best-known families continued the tradition where Saturday night short-track racing as entertainment was born and an economical Late Model division was first introduced.

11. Tammy Jo Kirk. In 1991, Kirk became the first female driver to run in NASCAR's Elite Division and in 1997, became the first female driver to compete in the NASCAR Camping World Truck Series, where she finished 20th in the points standings and seventh among 29 Rookie of the Year candidates.

10. Corinne Economaki. *National Speed Sport News* publisher Corinne Economaki worked her way up from selling ads, setting type, and doing billing for "America's Weekly Motorsports Authority" until she was eventually named publisher, following in the footsteps of her father—editor and publisher emeritus Chris Economaki.

9. Louise Smith. As the first woman to compete at NASCAR's highest level in 1949 (when the NASCAR Sprint Cup Series was known as NASCAR Strictly Stock), Smith was both a trailblazer and a novelty. Her highest finish in a NASCAR Grand National Division (now NASCAR Sprint Cup) race was 16th at Langhorne Speedway in 1949. She also often served as a willing spokesman and promoter of the sport.

8. Anne B. France. As NASCAR's first secretary and treasurer, and the first secretary and treasurer of the International Speedway Corporation—as well as the wife and partner of NASCAR founder Bill France Sr.—Anne France played a crucial role in the business of racing from the beginning and continued in that role throughout her entire life.

7. Patti Wheeler. As much as her father, Charlotte Motor Speedway President H. A. "Humpy" Wheeler, became synonymous with the track at Charlotte, Patti Wheeler became synonymous with NASCAR on TV. After serving as director of motorsports for TNN: The Nashville Network and chief executive of World Sports Enterprises, Wheeler started her own television production company, Wheeler Television, Inc. In 2010, she was named executive vice president of programming and production at SPEED.

6. Patty Moise. In 1986, Moise ran her first NASCAR Nationwide Series race, becoming the first woman to lead a NASCAR Nationwide event at Road Atlanta Speedway in 1987. She set many marks during her career, including the best-ever NASCAR Nationwide finish for a woman—second in the 1987 Road Atlanta race. She ran her last NASCAR Nationwide Series race in 1998, a season in which she made 19 starts. She also made five starts in NASCAR's premier series between 1987 and 1989.

5. Danica Patrick. In 2010, Patrick began racing part-time in the NASCAR Nationwide Series, driving the No. 7 GoDaddy.com Chevrolet Impala for JR Motorsports. In 2011, she became the first woman to lead a lap at Daytona International Speedway. She had her best career finish (fourth) in the NASCAR Nationwide Series on March 5, 2011, at the Las Vegas Motor Speedway. Her best finish—so far. In August 2010, Patrick announced that she would race in the NASCAR Nationwide Series full time in 2012.

4. Shawna Robinson. Over the course of her 17-year racing career, Robinson competed in both the NASCAR Nationwide Series and NASCAR Sprint Cup Series.

As a NASCAR Goody's Dash Series driver, Robinson was named Rookie of the Year following her debut season of 1988 and also captured the Most Popular Driver Award for two consecutive years. She became the first woman to win a pole in the series and the first woman to win a NASCAR touring event when she drove at New Asheville Speedway.

In the NASCAR Nationwide Series, she became the first woman to win a Coors Light Pole Award with her qualifying run at the Atlanta Motor Speedway, where she set a then-track-record speed of 174.330 mph. In the NASCAR Sprint Cup Series, where she made her debut in 2001, her best finish was 24th at the Daytona 500 that same year.

3. Janet Guthrie. A licensed pilot who at one point seriously considered becoming an astronaut, Guthrie was a natural for racing. In 1977, she became the first woman to compete in both the Indy 500 and the Daytona 500, where she finished 12th and was the top rookie of the race. Her best NASCAR Sprint Cup finish was sixth at Bristol Motor Speedway in 1977. Mostly, she served as the inspiration for all future female drivers.

2. Lisa France Kennedy. The daughter of the longtime President, CEO and Chairman of the Board Bill France Jr. and his wife, Betty Jane France, Lisa Kennedy has excelled as the CEO of International Speedway Corporation and Vice Chairwoman of NASCAR. In 2009, *Forbes* named her sport's most powerful woman.

1. Betty Jane France. The wife of the late Bill France Jr. and namesake of the Betty Jane France Humanitarian Award is well-known as the pioneer of charitable works in the NASCAR community. According to driver Rusty Wallace, she is the anchor of The NASCAR Foundation.

There can only be one winner in each race, and that's the main reason drivers compete—to win. But after that comes the top 10 finish. Wins pay the big bucks, but finishing consistently in the top 10 can put a driver in contention for a championship. And that, after all, is the big picture. When you look at this list of most consecutive top 10 finishes (all post-1990), you see championship-caliber drivers and teams.

17. Tony Stewart, 10 races. Race No. 13 (Dover, 2009) to Race No. 22 (Watkins Glen, 2009).

16. Terry Labonte, 10 races. Race No. 26 (Martinsville, 1996) to Race No. 4 (Atlanta, 1997).

15. Mark Martin, 10 races. Race No. 16 (Pocono, 1990) to Race No. 25 (North Wilkesboro, 1990).

14. Jeff Gordon, 10 races. Race No. 13 (Dover, 2007) to Race No. 22 (Watkins Glen, 2007).

13. Dale Jarrett, 11 races. Race No. 27 (Dover, 1999) to Race No. 3 (Las Vegas, 2000).

12. Morgan Shepherd, 12 races. Race No. 29 (Atlanta, 1989) to Race No. 11 (Dover, 1990).

11. Dale Earnhardt Sr., 12 races. Race No. 22 (Bristol, 1995) to Race No. 2 (Rockingham, 1996).

10. Dale Earnhardt Sr., 12 races. Race No. 14 (Michigan, 1990) to Race No. 25 (North Wilkesboro, 1990).

9. Tony Stewart, 13 races. Race No. 15 (Michigan, 2005) to Race No. 27 (New Hampshire, 2005).

8. Jimmie Johnson, 13 races. Race No. 31 (Charlotte, 2004) to Race No. 7 (Texas, 2005).

7. Bobby Labonte, 14 races. Race No. 25 (Richmond, 1999) to Race No. 4 (Atlanta, 2000).

6. Mark Martin, 14 races. Race No. 10 (Auto Club, 1998) to Race No. 23 (New Hampshire, 1998).

5. Jeff Gordon, 14 races. Race No. 14 (Michigan, 1995) to Race No. 27 (North Wilkesboro, 1995).

4. Dale Jarrett, 15 races. Race No. 10 (Auto Club, 2000) to Race No. 24 (Darlington, 2000).

3. Mark Martin, 16 races. Race No. 17 (Pocono, 1996) to Race No. 1 (Daytona, 1997).

2. Dale Jarrett, 19 races. Race No. 4 (Atlanta, 1999) to Race No. 22 (Michigan, 1999).

1. Jeff Gordon, 21 races. Race No. 14 (Michigan, 1998) to Race No. 1 (Daytona, 1999).

Drivers and crew chiefs know that races are won with a combination of skill, hard work, and plenty of luck. Since luck can often make or break a race, many drivers have developed superstitions over the years. Some of them are quirky; some can be explained away. But when a trip to Victory Lane sometimes boils down to tenths of a second, why tempt fate?

Superstitions aren't just about what not to do. When they coincide with a success-ful race day, certain acts can turn into a lucky routine a driver dare not break. For example, Sterling Marlin has eaten a bologna sandwich before some 800 starts. If Davey Allison watched a movie on a Friday and won the race on Sunday, he'd watch the same movie over and over until he lost a race.

Drivers are also known for the lucky charms they carry in their cars. Back in 1998, Dale Earnhardt Sr.—who had raced and lost 19 times at the Daytona 500—famously accepted a lucky penny from a fan, six-year-old Wessa Miller, who met her hero courtesy of the Make-A-Wish Foundation. Earnhardt glued the penny to his dash-board and finally won the race.

Here are an unlucky seven things many drivers consider bad luck.

7. Kissing a girl. Glenn "Fireball" Roberts swore that every time a girl kissed him before a race, he spun out, backed through a fence, or flipped end over end. The spell was broken in 1962 when—despite a prerace, good-luck kiss from the reigning Miss America, Mary Ann Mobley—Roberts won the Daytona 500.

6. Talk of winning. Don't say the word "win" before a race to Carl Edwards or his former NASCAR Nationwide Series crew chief, Brad Parrott. Don't talk about the tro-phy prior to the start with any driver.

5. Tails-up coins. Rusty Wallace and Todd Bodine, among others, refuse to pick up a coin unless it lands on "heads."

4. No. 13. The number 13 is, for many, synonymous with bad luck. Think Friday the 13th or how most big hotels don't have 13th floors. Despite the fact that a handful of drivers have been brave enough to drive a No. 13 car over the years (most recently Robbie Gordon in 2000, Hermie Sadler in 2001, and Joe Nemechek in 2006), in NASCAR, most drivers steer clear of the number. No competitor looks forward to starting 13th and even pit road has eliminated Stall 13 (instead, dubbing the slot, "12A").

3. Fifties. Speaking of money, many NASCAR drivers won't touch a $50 bill with a two-foot tire jack. Dale Earnhardt Sr. wouldn't touch a $50 bill. Sterling Marlin and car owners Eddie Wood and Richard Childress avoid them as well. And if you owe Tony Stewart money, make sure to pay him with $10s and $20s—anything but a $50 bill.

2. Green. Despite the fact that many green cars (the Planters car, the Gatorade car) have been winners over the years, the color of envy doesn't sit well with many NASCAR drivers. The literal explanation dates back to a 1920 accident in Beverly Hills, California, that killed two drivers, including defending Indianapolis 500 champion Gaston Chevrolet, who was driving a green car. Years later, Tim Richmond declined to drive a Folgers Decaffeinated Coffee car because of its green hue. Instead, he opted for the Folgers regular coffee car, which was bright red. The anti-green stigma is also connected to money and the negative connotations of selling out.

1. Peanut shells. Drivers say that these have been banned from shops since the 1930s, when peanut shells were scattered on five cars prior to a race and all five—and only those five—crashed before the day was done. There is also a story about one of Junior Johnson's drivers eating peanuts in the garage area prior to a race when an engine exploded. Just to be safe, many drivers won't touch the shells or the peanuts. Finding his team in a slump a few years ago, owner Robert Yates threw all the peanuts out of a vending machine and his team won the next race. You be the judge.

No one disputes that NASCAR is steeped in tradition. But perhaps Kyle Petty put it best when he said, "NASCAR still has a ton of tradition, it has just changed over the years to adapt to the modern era." Here are some examples that demonstrate that when it comes to stock car racing, as much as things change, they also stay the same.

7. The Coca-Cola July Race at Daytona. This always-anticipated race used to run every year on the 4th of July. But to accommodate as many fans as possible, NASCAR moved the race to the weekend closest to the July 4th.

6. Southern 500 at Darlington. This race is still part of the schedule, it's just no longer run on Labor Day weekend.

5. NASCAR Sprint Cup Series Championship Banquet. The annual championship banquet and awards ceremony used to always be held in New York City. But in 2009, NASCAR moved the season-ending gala to Las Vegas. (Miami is the site for the NASCAR Nationwide and NASCAR Camping World Truck Series Award Ceremony and Banquet.)

4. Final Race. In the past, the NASCAR Sprint Cup season finished at Atlanta Motor Speedway and the champion would be crowned there. But in 2001, the final race took place in New Hampshire for one year, before settling at Homestead-Miami Speedway in 2002, where it has been since. Ford Championship Weekend for all three national series takes place in Homestead, Florida.

3. Coca-Cola 600. Always on Memorial Day weekend—then and now—so fans can come to Charlotte Motor Speedway and make a good ol' all-American weekend out of it.

2. Mother's Day. Traditionally, races were never scheduled on Mother's Day so drivers could be home with their families. Then in 1986, the NASCAR Sprint All-Star Race, which was held in Atlanta, was run on Mother's Day. After that, Mother's Day was returned to an off-day on the NASCAR schedule with the NASCAR Sprint Cup Series competing on the Saturday before Mother's Day.

1. Easter. NASCAR has never run a race on Easter Sunday. Some things will never change.

Certain numbers have major significance to NASCAR fans. Here are some of the most important motorsports digits.

10. Two. The number of drivers to win seven NASCAR Sprint Cup Series championships (Richard Petty and Dale Earnhardt Sr.).

9. Three. The number emblazoned on the side of Dale Earnhardt Sr.'s famous black Chevy.

8. Five. The grand total (so far) of championships won by Jimmie Johnson.

7. Six. Total superspeedways in NASCAR (Auto Club, Daytona, Indianapolis, Michigan, Pocono, and Talladega).

6. Eleven. A pit crew's goal (in seconds) for an optimum pit stop.

5. Twelve. The number of drivers who qualify for the Chase for the NASCAR Sprint Cup.

4. Forty-eight. The maximum number of points a race winner can earn.

3. Two hundred. Total career wins by Richard Petty.

2. Five hundred. As in Daytona; also refers to other 500-mile races at other tracks, including Atlanta, Bristol, Darlington, and Phoenix.

1. 1948. The year NASCAR was born.

In racing, it's all about speed. So fans always want to know which track is the fastest. Every year, rule adjustments (for safety) and track improvements seem to change the answer. But here are the track speed records, as of the end of 2010.

5. Michigan International Speedway. In 2005, Ryan Newman set a track record on the smooth, wide surface on this track with a 194.232-mph lap.

4. Texas Motor Speedway. The Texas Motor Speedway was repaved in 2006 and—despite rule changes, such as the introduction of the spoiler earlier in the season—Brian Vickers took the Coors Light Pole Award at the track that year with a 196.235-mph lap that not only put him in front, but made Texas the fastest track of the era.

3. Atlanta Motor Speedway. In 1997, Geoffrey Bodine notched a 197.478-mph lap on the recently reconfigured track.

2. Daytona International Speedway. A few months prior to setting the mark at Talladega Superspeedway, Bill Elliott made history with a 210.364-mph lap while qualifying for the 1987 Great American Race. The introduction of restrictor plates in 1988 at Daytona and Talladega has since reduced speeds at these legendary tracks.

1. Talladega Superspeedway. In 1987, Bill Elliott clocked NASCAR's fastest lap to date (212.809 mph).

In 1985, the Charlotte Motor Speedway hosted the first NASCAR Sprint All-Star Race, a special event featuring race winners from the current and previous seasons in NASCAR's top series. Except for its second year—when it was run at the Atlanta Motor Speedway—the race has been a Charlotte, pre-Coca-Cola 600 tradition. Here are a few flashbacks of some of the most gripping All-Star race moments.

5. Only on SPEED (since 2007). SPEED secured exclusive broadcast rights for the race in 2007 and has been showcasing the event every year since.

4. Michael Waltrip's stunner (1996). During the early years of the event, only previous race winners competed in the All-Star race. Then, a qualifying event was added and the victor (or in 1996, the top five finishers) joined the field. In 1996, Michael Waltrip, who had not won a race in 309 starts, placed fifth in the qualifying run and became the unlikeliest All-Star driver. After starting last in the race, he took the lead in the final segment and held off Rusty Wallace to win it.

3. Darrell Waltrip's smoking gun (1985). Just 12 drivers, all previous race-season winners, competed in the inaugural 70-lap All-Star race. Things were pretty tame until—with only two laps left to go—Darrell Waltrip shot ahead of Harry Gant, who had led the previous 30 laps. Just as Waltrip crossed the finish line, white smoke billowed from the blown engine of his car.

Waltrip was accused of engaging the clutch to destroy (the possibly illegal) engine, to make inspections impossible. Waltrip protested. "No, no, no!" he said. "I was able to come on strong because [car owner] Junior [Johnson] got on the radio and inspired me. He asked me if I wanted $75,000 for second place or $200,000 for winning."

2. Davey Allison's dash and crash (1992). The race, billed as "One Hot Night" because it marked the debut of the new, groundbreaking lighting system at the Char-lotte track, was the scene of an awesome finish. During the fourth turn of the last lap, Kyle Petty forced front-runner Dale Earnhardt Sr. into a spin. Then Davey Allison, formerly third, edged past Petty to take the checkered flag. But just after clearing the finish line, Allison crashed. Despite some minor injuries race-winner Allison returned to Charlotte the following week to compete in the Coca-Cola 600.

1. Dale Earnhardt Sr.'s pass in the grass (1987). What became one of the most famous NASCAR video clips of all time wasn't even really a pass. With just shy of seven laps to go, Bill Elliott bumped leader Dale Earnhardt Sr., who proceeded to slice through the grassy area between the track and pit road and return to the track— without ever slowing down or surrendering his lead. A few laps later, Elliott is out with a cut-down tire and Earnhardt takes the checkered flag just ahead of Terry Labonte.

Strangest Autograph Requests

Like many famous folks, NASCAR drivers are often asked for their autographs. (Sometimes fans even ask SPEED Channel broadcasters for theirs, although that continues to mystify me.) NASCAR drivers are known to be among the most accessible of stars when it comes to signing. When a fan asks, they almost always say yes. When drivers sign something, it's usually a book, a poster, or a hat. Maybe a die-cast car. But fans have surprised drivers over the years by asking them to sign some unexpected things. Here are some of the strangest.

8. Puppy dog. Michael Waltrip once signed a Chihuahua.

7. And speaking of dogs. Greg Biffle says he gets many, many more requests for autographs when his dog, Foster, is with him.

6. Prosthetic leg. You never know how many folks at the race track have artificial limbs until you are asked to sign one. I guess it's not really any stranger than signing someone's cast.

5. Bald head. Almost every driver has signed one of these.

4. Breasts. Every driver has been asked to sign at least one.

3. Duck. According to Richard Petty, this is the most unusual thing he's ever put his Sharpie to.

2. Cars. Not that strange, but Rusty Wallace took it up a notch when he began making a habit of signing people's new cars at his car dealership in Tennessee.

1. Tires. Again, not that strange considering the link between tires, cars, and drivers. But it has to be cumbersome for a fan to carry a huge tire around in pursuit of an autograph. It's not exactly discreet.

In May 2010, the 150,000-square-foot, NASCAR Hall of Fame opened for business in Charlotte, North Carolina. With more than 40,000 square feet of exhibit space, dozens of interactive exhibits, and more than 1,000 authentic artifacts, the museum immediately established itself as a racing fan's paradise.

The most impressive thing about the NASCAR Hall of Fame is the inductees themselves. The inaugural class of NASCAR greats consisted of Dale Earnhardt Sr., Bill France Sr., Bill France Jr., Junior Johnson, and Richard Petty. The 2011 class included Bobby Allison, Ned Jarrett, Bud Moore, David Pearson, and Lee Petty, followed by Richie Evans, Dale Inman, Darrell Waltrip, Glen Wood, and Cale Yarborough in 2012.

Besides the legends, the NASCAR Hall of Fame is home to some really cool stuff. Here are some favorites.

15. Richard Petty's 1967 Plymouth. This electric blue Plymouth Belvedere carried the King to Victory Lane in 27 of 48 races during a 1967 season that included a record 10 wins in a row for Petty.

14. Darrell Waltrip's No. 11 Buick. Waltrip drove this car to NASCAR premier series titles in 1981 and 1982.

13. Jeff Gordon's first racing helmet. The first of many for Gordon, who started racing quarter midgets at age five.

12. Ned Jarrett's CBS blazer. A memento from Gentleman Ned's initial switch from driver to prognosticator.

11. Davey Allison's boots, hat, and bow and arrow. Gear representing Allison's second favorite activity.

10. Unocal 76 spotter ball. This enormous spotter ball, one of four Daytona International Speedway originals (circa 1969), arrived in Charlotte in sections and took three days to install.

9. Smokey Yunick's wooden templates. The real deal from a legendary mechanic and car builder.

8. Richie Evans's No. 61 modified car. The ride of the nine-time NASCAR Modified Tour champion.

7. Richard Petty's Presidential Medal of Freedom. A medal fit for the King.

6. I-Racing simulators. The next best thing to driving a race car for real.

5. Brick pavers lining Ceremonial Plaza. Personalized bricks pave the way into the NASCAR Hall of Fame.

4. Glory Road. Fans are invited to walk on the surface of this banked ramp simulating the turns of various race tracks, including Talladega Superspeedway and its high banks of up to 33 degrees.

3. Race Week. Visitors take time out to practice pit stops, call a race as a broadcaster, and prowl around a working NASCAR team hauler.

2. NASCAR'S greatest finishes. The interactive jukebox features 50 of NASCAR's classic finales.

1. Moonshine Still Handcrafted by Junior Johnson. Proof of NASCAR's white-lightning roots.

We often say that NASCAR is not the witness protection program and the idea is to get noticed. As a driver, one of the best means to that end is to display an eye-catching paint scheme on your car. Here are some of the most memorable designs from races past.

13. Troops first. The first appearance of special, one-off paint schemes can be traced to an R.J. Reynolds promotion at the 1991 Daytona 500, where five drivers (No. 7 Alan Kulwicki, No. 18 Greg Sacks, No. 24 Mickey Gibbs, No. 71 Dave Marcis, and No. 88 Buddy Baker) ran with paint schemes saluting different branches of the military (army, navy, air force, coast guard, and marines) to honor U.S. military personnel serving in Operation Desert Storm.

12. Name tags. At the Charlotte race in May 2009, Jimmie Johnson's patriotic No. 48 Lowe's Impala SS carried the names of 12,548 Lowe's employees who are military veterans or reservists.

11. Creative driver. When Dale Jr. moved from DEI to Hendricks Motorsports for the 2008 season, he designed the effervescent paint scheme for his first AMP Energy Drink car.

10. Creative fans. Over the years, several lucky contest winners have seen their paint scheme ideas come to life courtesy of sponsor contests, such as Kodak's Ink Ryan's Ride contest for Ryan Newman's No. 12 Dodge in 2007 (won by Raymond Vanderlinden of Springfield, Missouri) or the Little Tikes Special Paint Scheme Contest for Kurt Busch's No. 97 Ford in 2002 (won by Little Tikes employee Pat Cieplinski).

9. Saving face. Occasionally, famous faces (including those of cartoon characters, such as Fred Flintstone and Superman) appear on cars. In an unusual twist in the late 1990s, Richard Petty's likeness ran on the hood of his own car when it was driven by John Andretti. Other famous painted faces to appear include Andy Griffith, in honor of the 50th anniversary of *The Andy Griffith Show* in 2010, and John Wayne, in honor of the John Wayne Cancer Institute.

8. Moving pictures. Although movies had been promoted on cars before (*Jurassic Park* on the No. 24 DuPont Chevy in 1997, *The Blues Brothers* on the No. 44 Hot Wheels Pontiac in 1998, *Ali* on the No. 9 Dodge in 2001, etc.), Bobby Labonte's No. 18 Interstate Batteries Chevy's 2004 paint scheme promoting Mel Gibson's controversial *The Passion of the Christ* movie paved the way for any and all feature film sponsors. Since then, we've seen many more, including *Star Wars Episode III: Revenge of the Sith*, which rode to victory with Jeff Gordon at Talledega in 2005.

7. Sports cars. Sports teams and big sporting events have been given shout-outs on race cars dozens of times over the years, including the Boston Red Sox (Carl Edwards and David Ragan) and the Olympics (Dale Earnhardt Sr., Kasey Kahne). One particularly memorable tie-in was with Baltimore Orioles star Cal Ripken Jr., who played his final Major League Baseball game in 2001. To celebrate the event, Ripken served as Grand Marshal and namesake of the MBNA Cal Ripken Jr. 400, in which Bobby Labonte drove a Ripken-themed Pontiac Grand Prix in his honor.

6. Track charity. A list of every NASCAR charitable venture and corresponding race car paint scheme would fill a phone book. Standouts over the years include Dale Jarrett's 1999 reversed-color Ford in honor of breast cancer awareness and John Andretti's 2001 Dodge covered with painted handprints, each representing a dollar donated to Victory Junction. More recent charitable painted ventures include Greg Biffle's recurring American Red Cross scheme and Denny Hamlin's March of Dimes scheme at Texas Motor Speedway in 2011.

5. Race rock. Rock bands such as KISS, Barenaked Ladies, Metallica, and Red Hot Chili Peppers have rolled in on cars over the years, often as part of events such as the Chevy Rock & Roll 400. Country stars, too. Sterling Marlin ran with a Brooks & Dunn/Coors Light paint scheme for years and cars such as Joe Nemechek's Charlie Daniels Band Chevy have become commonplace.

4. Happy anniversary. Always the trendsetter, Dale Earnhardt Sr. made a splash in 1995 when he swapped his traditional black car for a silver-painted ride (nicknamed Silverwrench, Silver Select, or Silver Bullet, depending on whom you asked) in honor of the former series sponsor's silver anniversary. Later, during his 1997 season, Darrell Waltrip celebrated his own silver anniversary as a NASCAR driver by running with a special "Chrome Car."

3. Less is more. After the terrorist attacks of 9/11, virtually every driver paid tribute to those who died on that terrible day by changing the paint scheme of his car for the next race on the schedule. American flags were everywhere, from Sterling Marlin's No. 40 God Bless America Dodge to Michael Waltrip's No.15 NAPA Chevrolet. But Ken Schrader stood out by doing less. His No. 36 M&Ms car was swathed only in the American flag; in a classy move, the M&Ms logo and all references to associate sponsors had been removed.

2. Throwback rides. Often, paint schemes are nods to the past. In 2006, Dale Earnhardt Jr. ran a Budweiser throwback scheme on Father's Day to honor his grandfather, Ralph Earnhardt. That same year, he also ran an all-black, Intimidator-themed scheme to celebrate the induction of his father, Dale Earnhardt Sr., into the International Motorsports Hall of Fame. During Rusty Wallace's "Last Call" tour in his final season of 2005, he ran with the original Miller Genuine Draft black-and-gold paint scheme from the 1991–1995 era. And in 2007 at Michigan International Speedway, 11 Team Chevy drivers (Ward Burton, Dale Earnhardt Jr., Jeff Gordon, Jimmie Johnson, Mark Martin, Casey Mears, Paul Menard, Tony Raines, Martin Truex Jr., Scott Wimmer, and J. J. Yeley) rode with paint schemes commemorating the 50th anniversary of the 1957 Chevrolet.

1. Quick change. Perhaps the best paint scheme ever was on Jeff Gordon's 1998 NASCAR Sprint All-Star Race car. Created with ChromaLusion paint, a DuPont product that actually changes colors, the car shifted from gold to metallic purple to bright copper as it went by. Broadcasters had to remind viewers not to adjust their TV sets.

When a driver wins a NASCAR Sprint Cup Series race, he doesn't necessarily take home an actual cup. Each track awards its own unique trophy and because it's NASCAR, the bigger and more outrageous, the better. Here, in no particular order (because it's tough to compare grandfather clocks to guitars), are some of the most unusual prizes given trackside.

19. Harley Davidson (Road America). What driver wouldn't want a brand new Harley?

18. Guitar (Nashville Superspeedway). The prize for NASCAR Camping World Truck and NASCAR Nationwide Series race winners at Nashville is a one-of-a-kind, Gibson guitar. Buddy Baker won one back in the day, but wondered what he'd do with it. "I was like a pig with a wristwatch," Baker said.

In 2009, Kyle Busch stirred up a stink when he smashed his Les Paul Gibson original, which was hand painted by artist Sam Bass. Busch said he was breaking it into pieces to share with his crew. Bass said he wished he'd given Busch a replica, rather than a piece of art that took eight weeks to create.

17. Guitar (Richmond International Raceway). At the Chevy Rock & Roll 400, the winner was awarded a Paul Reed Smith guitar on a 70-pound base.

16. Grandfather clock (Martinsville Speedway). The tradition of awarding an actual working grandfather clock (which chimes "God Bless America" and "America the Beautiful") began back in the early 1960s when the founder of Martinsville Speedway, H. Clay Earles, sought out an unusual prize and found what he was looking for courtesy of a local furniture manufacturer, Ridgeway Clock Company.

15. Mounted wildlife (Atlanta Motor Speedway). When Bass Pro Shops was the title sponsor of the Atlanta race, the prize was an enormous mounted grizzly bear, giant large-mouth bass, or a pair of bald eagles. Friends visiting Tony Stewart's trophy room might wonder whether he bagged a bear in Atlanta or won a race.

14. Pair of cowboy boots (Texas Motor Speedway). Boots for a prize makes sense in Texas. But these are really, really big, hand-carved, mounted cowboy boots. And most people just bronze their baby booties.

13. Miles the Monster Trophy (Dover International Speedway). Monster Mile, Monster Trophy. 'Nuff said. But, there's more. Just prior to the celebration in Victory Lane, a replica of the winner's car is placed in the monster's hand. And, there's a 46-foot-tall statue of Miles, the mascot monster featured on the trophy, outside the track.

12. LifeLock.com 400 Trophy (Kansas Speedway). For everyone who has ever received a gift and said, "I love it. What is it?" It's been called a can opener, a whale's tale, or a flapping bird. But it's actually a sculpture called *Soaring* by a Canadian artist.

11. Pep Boys Trophy (Atlanta Motor Speedway). It was a little cartoony for a trophy awarded to a guy who just drove 500 miles, but at least each of the three Pep Boys had a function: one held a tire; one held a battery; and the other held a winner's cup.

10. The Aaron's 499 Trophy (Talladega Superspeedway). Maybe the folks at Aaron's heard the cloud atop their former trophy compared to George Washington's powdered wig, because the new, more traditional Sam Bass-designed trophy features a driver standing on a black-stained walnut base sculpted in the shape of Talladega's 2.66-mile, tri-oval track.

9. Elvis Trophy (Memphis Motorsports Park). Elvis sightings happen everywhere, especially in Memphis, where from 2005 to 2009 lucky winners of the NASCAR Camping World Truck Series and NASCAR Nationwide Series races took home the Elvis Trophy.

8. Cactus Trophy (Phoenix International Raceway). What else would you expect from a track in the middle of the Arizona desert? Jeff Gordon, who was thrilled to bring the enormous cactus home in 2011, said he kind of wished it was small enough to carry around.

7. Championship belt (Las Vegas Motor Speedway). What happens in Vegas, stays in Vegas. Except if you happened to win at the Las Vegas Motor Speedway. When that happened, you used to bring home a big, gaudy $3,000 title belt encrusted with gold, diamonds, and rubies from the Fight Capitol of the World.

6. The Champion's Cabernet Wine Goblet (Infineon Raceway). In Victory Lane, thirsty race winners are known to drink Coke, Gatorade, or even champagne. But when in wine country, the victor is handed a foot-high goblet filled with fine cabernet to accompany the trophy, which consists of a three-liter wine bottle and five wooden casks. When in the Sonoma Valley . . .

5. The Bristol Cup (Bristol Motor Speedway). If bigger is better, then this four-foot-tall, 50-pound trophy topped with a politically incorrect winged woman is the best.

4. Charlotte Motor Speedway Trophy (Charlotte Motor Speedway). The original trophy was so heavy that Bobby Allison, the first driver to win this prize in 1981, actually dropped to his knees when it was handed to him. It's since been hollowed out, so that it now weighs in at a more manageable 22 pounds.

3. The Brick (Indianapolis Motor Speedway). Drivers dream of winning this trophy from the famed Brickyard. It's a simple brick resting atop a base made of gold, sterling silver, and alloy aluminum. As traditional as kissing the bricks.

2. The Harley J. Earl Trophy (Daytona International Speedway). One of the most coveted prizes in NASCAR, this trophy consists of a replica of General Motors designer Harley J. Earl's 1954 Firebird mounted on a black tri-oval shaped base.

1. NASCAR Sprint Cup Series Championship Trophy. Ultimately, this is the trophy every driver wants.

There wasn't always Twitter, Facebook, and the Web. Fans used to have to wait until writers filed their stories and they appeared in the paper the next day or in a magazine the following week or month. Hundreds of great motorsports writers have covered NASCAR over the years. But here are some who made a lasting impact and were always worth the wait in the pre-Twitter world.

7. Tom Jensen. His past and present journalistic posts include editor in chief of SPEED.com, senior NASCAR editor at *Racer* and contributing editor for Truck-Series.com. The past president of the NMPA and winner of the NMPA George Cunningham Award, Jensen is also a book author.

6. Leigh Montville. He was never a NASCAR beat writer, but Montville wrote several great racing features as a staff writer for *Sports Illustrated* over the years and a fantastic page-turner on Dale Earnhardt Sr., which was released in 2001.

5. Tom Higgins. This longtime *Charlotte Observer* writer (1964–1997) was given NASCAR's Award of Excellence in 1996. In 2011, he was inducted into the Hall of Fame by the National Motorsports Press Association (NMPA), which had awarded him the NMPA George Cunningham Award (as Writer of the Year) in 1987.

4. Steve Waid. The quintessential motorsports journalist, Waid began as a reporter in Virginia for the *Martinsville Bulletin* back in 1972, and then worked for 10 years as the motorsports writer for the *Roanoke Times & World News*. After that, he joined the staff of *Grand National Scene*, a small NASCAR weekly, and later became a magazine publisher for *NASCAR Scene* and *NASCAR Illustrated*.

Waid has received numerous honors, including the NMPA George Cunningham Award and the Henry T. McLemore Award for outstanding lifetime contributions to motorsports. He also served as NMPA president for 12 years.

Waid has also been a fixture on syndicated radio shows over the years and talked NASCAR on TV as a cohost of *NASCAR This Morning* on FOX. He also contributes commentary on motorsportsunplugged.com.

3. David Poole. Longtime *Charlotte Observer* writer David Poole, who suddenly passed away at age 50 in 2009, was a fixture at the race track for many years. NASCAR fans counted on his opinions and insights into the racing world, which he offered in his newspaper column and as a cohost of *The Morning Drive* on Sirius. The four-time winner of the NMPA George Cunningham Award also authored several stock car racing books.

2. Godwin Kelly. From his post of motorsports editor at the *Daytona Beach News-Journal*, Kelly has covered NASCAR from its birthplace since 1982. He has also found time to write several great racing books.

1. Mike Hembree. This writer has been covering motorsports for different outlets (*NASCAR Scene*, SPEED.com) for decades. Hembree has written or cowritten 12 books on NASCAR, and has won numerous national, regional, and state awards for writing and reporting—including the NMPA George Cunningham Award, which he has won six times. In 2008, he was named the winner of the Henry T. McLemore Award for career achievements in motorsports journalism.

Drivers say some pretty wild things in the heat of the moment. Come to think of it, they say some pretty wild things even when the moment isn't so hot. Here are some racing quotes that bear repeating.

23. Janet Guthrie, when asked if, as a woman, she had the strength to drive a race car. "You drive the car, you don't carry it."

22. Buddy Baker, on newcomer Dale Earnhardt Sr. during his NASCAR Sprint Cup Series rookie season of 1980. "He's got more nerve than a sore tooth."

21. Geoffrey Bodine, on restrictor-plate racing at Talladega. "I think it's the most awful, dirtiest, nastiest, most dangerous racing in the whole wide world."

20. Adam Petty, on his place in racing's legendary Petty family. "My grandfather is the King, my dad is the Prince. I guess that makes me the butler."

19. Dale Earnhardt Sr., when asked about his high-contact fifth win at Talledega. "God created bumpers and . . . bumpers were made for bumping."

18. Glenn "Fireball" Roberts, after mixing it up with Fred Lorenzen at Martinsville in 1962. "I guess all we proved is that the back end of a Pontiac is tougher than the front end of a Ford."

17. Chad Knaus, crew chief for Jimmie Johnson. "Drive it like you stole it, Homie."

16. Darrell Waltrip. "If you don't cheat, you look like an idiot; if you cheat and don't get caught, you look like a hero; if you cheat and get caught, you look like a dope. Put me where I belong."

15. Junior Johnson, when he was accused of cheating back in the 1960s. "They haven't caught me if I am."

14. Anonymous. "If you ain't cheatin', you ain't tryin'."

13. Buddy Baker, when asked about driving through a jumble of wrecked cars and a curtain of thick smoke. "It's amazing what you can do with your eyes closed."

12. Kyle Petty. "If driving a race car was easy, then women and children would be doing it. Oh, wait. Women and children are doing it."

11. David Pearson, when asked in 1965 which race he preferred to win. "Charlotte. Because it pays the most."

10. Richard Petty. "Racing is where you run up there and beat on someone, and you get by them, and then you go on to the next guy."

9. Cale Yarborough. "Driving a race car is like dancing with a chainsaw."

8. Ernest Hemingway. "Auto racing, bullfighting, and mountain climbing are the only real sports. All others are games."

7. Owner Richard Childress, after Dale Earnhardt Sr. finally won the Daytona 500 in 1998. "Even Dale, who hates cigars, took a few puffs. So I saw him do two things that day that I had not seen him do before."

6. Ralph Earnhardt. "There's only one lap you want to lead, and that's the last lap."

5. Richard Petty. "No one wants to quit when he's losing and no one wants to quit when he's winning."

4. Dale Earnhardt Sr. "Second place is just the first loser."

3. Alan Kulwicki. "First you learn how to drive fast. Next, you learn to drive fast in traffic. Then, you learn how to do it for 500 miles."

2. Louise Smith, NASCAR's first woman driver, on race-car driving for a career in the 1940s and 1950s. "Sometimes it seemed like the more you drove the less money you had. I remember one time Buck Baker and Lee Petty and I had to put our money together just to split a hot dog and a Coke."

1. Darrell Waltrip. "Boogity, boogity, boogity. Let's go racing!"

Most of the funny things that race car driver and NASCAR RaceDay and Victory Lane cohost Kenny Wallace says are not fit for print. Some of the funny things he says have actually made it onto national TV. A few haven't. In my opinion, all of these are classics.

3. On the F-1 race in Bahrain. "Where is Bahrain? I never was too good at geometry."

2. On six races to go in the Chase. "Look fans, I can count 'em on one hand."

1. On the multitude of bloggers writing about NASCAR. "Most people with those Web bloggers are just fat guys sitting in their parents' basement eating potato chips."

My Mother's Favorite Things About NASCAR

Full disclosure: When I was growing up, the Roberts family never watched NASCAR on TV. We weren't really a motorsports family. But later, Mom and Dad watched every show and started following NASCAR religiously when their youngest son was working at SPEED.

Although she now has a pretty good grasp of racing in general, Mom—"Ma," as my kids call her—is not exactly a stickler for details, as evidenced by her list of NASCAR favorites.

6. Favorite driver. "That boy who almost came in second last year." (She meant Jamie McMurray.)

5. Favorite personality on *NASCAR RaceDay*. "I like Kenny and the boy with the ponytail." (I think she left someone out. Also, don't tell Kyle Petty that when she does remember his name is "Kyle" she usually refers to him as "Kyle Busch.")

4. Favorite thing about watching races. "I enjoy looking at their suits; all the different designs."

3. Least favorite thing about watching races on TV. "It's noisy, but I can always turn the sound down."

2. Favorite track to visit. "Charlotte, because the nice people at SPEED always give us a place to sit in the shade while my son does his TV show."

1. Ma's question when I made a joke about making a living watching a bunch of guys turn left all day. "Why do they only turn left?"

In the world of team sports, athletes are often identified with their uniform numbers. In NASCAR, the number of a driver's car is what's important. Some—No. 3, No. 43, No.11, No. 24, No. 48, No. 21—are legendary. Others—No. 88, No. 2, No. 17, No. 14—are well on their way to becoming legendary. And then there are the 24 car numbers—No. 02, No. 03, No. 04, No. 05, No. 08, No. 35, No. 36, No. 50, No. 57, No. 61, No. 63, No. 65, No. 67, No. 68, No. 69, No. 70, No. 74, No. 76, No. 79, No. 82, No. 84, No. 93, No. 94, and No. 95—that have zero wins to their credit.

As of May 2011, a total of 103 different car numbers have been winners in NASCAR Sprint Cup Series races. Here's how the number of wins line up with the numbers on the car doors. (Note: thanks to Jayski.com for the bulk of the numbers crunching for this list.)

10. Tenth all-time wins by number: No. 88. This car number is currently driven by Dale Earnhardt Jr., who was previously identified with No. 8. It has won 66 races in its history, beginning with Buck Baker, who drove the No. 88 in 1954.

9. Ninth all-time wins by number: No. 42. With drivers from Lee Petty to Juan Pablo Montoya behind the wheel, the No. 42 has won 69 times.

8. Eighth all-time wins by number: No. 2. This car, a winner since the 1950s, has visited Victory Lane 70 times, most recently accompanied by driver Brad Keselowski.

7. Seventh all-time wins by number: No. 28. This car, last driven to Victory Lane by Ricky Rudd in 2002, has 76 wins to its credit.

6. Sixth all-time wins by number: No. 6. The first driver to win in the No. 6 was Marshall Teague back in 1951; the last was David Ragan, who took it to its 83rd win in 2011.

5. Fifth all-time wins by number: No. 24. Jeff Gordon pretty much owns the No. 24, having won with it 85 times.

4. Fourth all-time wins by number: No. 21. Rookie Trevor Bayne drove it for the win at the 2011 Daytona 500. That was his first visit to Victory Lane on any track, but the No. 21 had been there 90 times before.

3. Third all-time wins by number: No. 3. The famed No. 3 is third with 97 wins, most of them by Dale Earnhardt Sr. He was the last driver to win in the No. 3 car in 2000; the first was Dick Rathmann in 1954.

2. Second all-time wins by number: No. 11. Drivers Ned Jarrett, Cale Yarborough, Darrell Waltrip, Bill Elliott and Denny Hamlin (among others) have won 197 times with lucky No. 11.

1. Most all-time wins by number: No. 43. The famed "43" is first with 198 wins. Lee Petty was the first to win in the No. 43, and later, Richard Petty made it the most famous number in racing. It's interesting to note, though, that en route to becoming the King, Richard Petty also won in the No. 41 and No. 42 cars. The last driver to win in the No. 43 was John Andretti in 1999.

The Weirdest Things Rutledge Wood Has Done for TV

Anyone who has watched *NASCAR RaceDay, Trackside* or *NASCAR Smarts* knows that roving reporter Rutledge Wood will do just about anything in the name of quality television. Here are Rutledge's personal picks for his most outrageous on-air antics.

6. Conducted interviews wearing an Appalachian State football uniform. Wouldn't have been that outrageous, but the interviewees were residents of Michigan directly following their Wolverines suffering the biggest upset in the history of University of Michigan football at the hands of App State. Unfortunately, things got a little dicey in the crowd.

5. Ate vegemite with Marcos Ambrose, and then threw up. Ambrose hails from Australia, so Americans often ask him about vegemite, a dark brown yeast extract that Aussies spread on toast. Rutledge tried it and promptly threw up for his first on-air vomit.

4. Ate a 22-inch chili cheese dog at Auto Club Speedway. And didn't throw up. After eating one of these enormous dogs on live TV, Rutledge felt sick but didn't actually get sick. Only later did a producer tell him he really didn't have to eat the whole thing; through the magic of editing, they could have made it look like he did.

3. Set up a kiddie pool at Pocono Raceway to host a pool party. The weather report called for freezing rain, so even though he invited all the drivers, only Michael Waltrip showed up. Waltrip never misses a party.

2. Dressed up as Michael Waltrip on Halloween and knocked on the door of Waltrip's motor home. Priceless.

1. Asked *Dukes of Hazzard* actor John Schneider an awkward question regarding Daisy Duke. In the course of interviewing Schneider (who played "Bo Duke" in the original *Dukes of Hazzard* TV series and was scheduled to sing the National Anthem at the 2007 Atlanta race), Rutledge asked him if he'd ever hooked up with Catherine Bach, the actress who played Daisy Duke on the TV show. "It's not like you were related to each other in real life," Rutledge said. Schneider respectfully declined to answer. A History Channel producer saw the piece and laughed so hard he offered Rutledge his current position as cohost of *Top Gear*.

What Makes NASCAR an All-American Pastime?

Perhaps *NBC Nightly News* anchor Brian Williams put it best when he said, "The sport of NASCAR is a reflection of America, a place with a real romantic side, which I see in hard-working people asking to be entertained at a small race track on a Friday or Saturday night."

Whether the venue is a small, local dirt track or a monolith such as Indianapolis Motor Speedway, Americans love stock car racing.

Baseball may be America's pastime, and a certain gridiron sport may have the edge on total TV viewership, but as an overall package, NASCAR may be the purest form of American entertainment. Here are 15 reasons to back up that statement:

15. The scene. Tailgating is an American specialty. When it comes to NASCAR, the party stretches out for days, with far more impressive and family-friendly tailgating than any other sport can claim. The fare—from hot dogs to funnel cakes—is also classic Americana.

14. The patriotism. It's everywhere on the track, from "God Bless America" played at prerace concerts to flags flying trackside. Before the engines fire, the National Anthem is played as fans, drivers, and crew members take off their caps and hold their hands over their hearts.

13. The noise. Races are loud, fast, and colorful. What could be more American than that?

12. The holidays. Is it a coincidence that many of the biggest events fall on Memorial Day and the Fourth of July?

11. Miss USA. Kristen Dalton, who was crowned Miss USA in 2009, later wore a NASCAR-themed outfit as her national costume in the Miss Universe Pageant. She also sang the National Anthem at the Coca-Cola 600 that same year.

10. The traveling show. Drivers and fans tote their families from track to track and partake of American pastimes such as camping, picnicking, and cheering loud and long.

9. The tracks. Venues hosting NASCAR Sprint Cup Series races, such as Daytona International Speedway hosting the Great American Race, are major landmarks in this country.

8. The fans. Jim Cramer, host of CNBC's *Mad Money*, described NASCAR and its fans as a true cross section of America. Fans come from all walks of life, and on race weekends, they celebrate their sport in a big, American way, with an average of approximately 100,000 of their closest friends at any given race.

7. The military. As Bill France Jr. once said, "NASCAR fans are the kind of Americans who fight and win wars." Servicemen are frequently honored at races as special guests or even as the namesake of a particular event. At many races, fans look skyward to see spine-tingling flyovers, courtesy of the Blue Angels or the Stealth Bomber.

6. The sponsors. NASCAR is a display of good ol' American capitalism. More than 100 *Fortune* 500 companies sponsor stock car racing to the tune of millions of dollars, and drivers are proud to stump for their backers.

5. The equity. Although bigger, better-funded teams always have an advantage, every driver has a chance to win at any given race.

4. The reward. In NASCAR, drivers are paid when they win; pay for performance is a fair and very American concept. (As the King said, "Run better, get more money.")

3. The drivers. Yes, they're heroes. But they're also regular people. In NASCAR, the common man does uncommon things. That's about as American as you can get.

2. The crews. The ingenuity and work ethic of the crews—from head mechanics and engineers to tire changers and jackmen—is all-American.

1. The cars. Americans have enjoyed a longtime love affair with the automobile, and most cars seen on a NASCAR track were built in the good ol' U.S.A.

All-Time Laps Led

Every race car driver strives to run at the front of the pack. Leading laps doesn't guarantee a driver will win a race, but no one argues that up front is a very good place to be. Because NASCAR awards bonus points for leading laps (one point to any driver that leads a lap and an additional bonus point for the driver who leads the most laps in a race), there is even more incentive to push for the lead.

In 2010, a record-setting 55 drivers led at least one lap—the most since 2005 and 2007, when 51 drivers did it. It's an accomplishment to lead even one lap in a NASCAR Sprint Cup Series race. But here are the 35 drivers who've chalked up the most lead laps during their entire careers (through August 27, 2011).

35. Davey Allison, 4,971.

34. Herb Thomas, 5,390.

33. Buck Baker, 5,420.

32. Ernie Irvan, 5,469.

31. Fireball Roberts, 5,975.

30. Tim Flock, 6,262.

29. Matt Kenseth, 6,288.

28. Neil Bonnett, 6,376.

27. Jeff Burton, 6,413.

26. Dale Earnhardt Jr., 6,762.

25. Benny Parsons, 6,828.

24. Kyle Busch, 6,833.

23. Kurt Busch, 6,926.

22. Dale Jarrett, 7,052.

21. Terry Labonte, 7,066.

20. Ricky Rudd, 7,974.

19. Fred Lorenzen, 8,099.

18. Harry Gant, 8,362.

17. Geoffrey Bodine, 8,683.

16. Ned Jarrett, 9,468.

15. Buddy Baker, 9,741.

14. Bill Elliott, 11,419.

13. Tony Stewart, 11,527.

12. Jimmie Johnson, 11,585.

11. Mark Martin, 12,535.

10. Junior Johnson, 12,643.

9. Bobby Isaac, 13,200.

8. Rusty Wallace, 19,972.

7. Jeff Gordon, 22,225.

6. Darrell Waltrip, 23,134.

5. David Pearson, 25,159.

4. Dale Earnhardt, 25,683.

3. Bobby Allison, 27,344.

2. Cale Yarborough, 31,627.

1. Richard Petty, 51,695.

NASCAR's roots are in the American South. But, in truth, great drivers from all over the country compete at tracks every week. America's love affair with automobile racing is a truly nationwide phenomenon. Here are some of the best drivers from far-flung places to drive in America's top tier of motorsports.

15. Clint Bowyer (Emporia, Kansas). The 2008 NASCAR Nationwide Series champ and subsequent Chase for the NASCAR Sprint Cup contender first put himself on the racing map by winning the 2000 Modified Championship at Thunderhill Speedway in Mayetta, Kansas.

14. Matt Kenseth (Cambridge, Wisconsin). Before he was a NASCAR Sprint Cup Series champion, Matt Kenseth won dozens of races in Wisconsin, including a victory at age 19 in Lacrosse, Wisconsin, that made him the youngest winner in ARTGO Challenge history. In 1994, he also became the youngest driver to win the Miller Genuine Draft National championships.

13. Jeff Gordon (Vallejo, California). At age five, Gordon learned to race on a makeshift track that his stepfather built near their home in California. The family moved to Pittsboro, Indiana, so 13-year-old Jeff could race sprints. Championships at Bloomington Speedway and a title at Eldora Speedway set the course for the future four-time NASCAR Sprint Cup champ.

12. Jimmie Johnson (El Cajon, California). The repeat NASCAR Sprint Cup champion cut his teeth (sometimes, literally) jumping motorcycles and driving off-road vehicles, trucks, hot rods, and buggies in the California desert.

11. Tony Stewart (Columbus, Indiana). Stewart started out in Indiana racing go-karts at age eight. After becoming one of NASCAR's top stars, Stewart made the ultimate nod to his roots when he purchased and moved back into his Indiana boyhood home.

10. Greg Biffle (Vancouver, Washington). Biffle grew up working on cars and racing at local tracks near his hometown. After winning races on short tracks throughout the Northwest, he was bound for NASCAR's top series.

9. Kasey Kahne (Enumclaw, Washington). At age eight, Kahne started racing four-wheelers on the eighth-of-a-mile-long dirt track his father built in his "backyard"—which consisted of more than 50 wooded acres. The future NASCAR Sprint Cup star honed his skills by spinning out on the ice during cold Northwest winters.

8. Carl Edwards (Columbia, Missouri). Long before becoming a NASCAR Sprint Cup driver, Edwards drove go-karts and dune buggies around his childhood (and current) hometown of Columbia, Missouri.

7. Jamie McMurray (Joplin, Missouri). McMurray grew up racing go-karts in Missouri and competed in every possible go-kart series around the country before switching to stock cars. In 2010, he won two of the biggest races on the NASCAR Sprint Cup circuit, the Daytona 500 and Brickyard 400.

6. Kevin Harvick (Bakersfield, California). This Californian made his way from go-karts and NASCAR Late Model events around Southern California to the NASCAR K&N Pro Series West, NASCAR Camping World Truck Series, and NASCAR Nationwide Series before he started notching wins in NASCAR Sprint Cup competition.

5. Ryan Newman (South Bend, Indiana). Before he left Indiana to hit the NASCAR Sprint Cup circuit, this Hoosier graduated with a degree in Vehicle Structure Engineering from Purdue University in West Lafayette, Indiana. Newman also competed in midget races and drove in USAC (United States Auto Club) open-wheel series races, winning the USAC Silver Crown division in 1999.

4. Alan Kulwicki (Greenfield, Wisconsin). Before becoming one of NASCAR's 50 Greatest Drivers, Kulwicki, who grew up just a few blocks from the Milwaukee Mile race track, began racing go-karts at age 13. He graduated to stock cars and competed on dirt oval tracks, such as Cedarburg and Hales Corner Speedway, before moving on to paved tracks and, eventually, NASCAR's top series.

3. Ricky Craven (Newburgh, Maine). Craven's road to NASCAR began in 1982 at Unity Raceway in Unity, Maine, with two wins and the Rookie of the Year title. Other wins at New England tracks paved his way to the American-Canadian Tour and the NASCAR Nationwide Series, followed by NASCAR Sprint Cup competition.

2. Regan Smith (Cato, New York). The 2008 NASCAR Sprint Cup Rookie of the Year started out racing quarter-midget cars (microds) in and around Syracuse and at other New York State tracks. After collecting the World Karting Association (WKA) Championship in 1996 and winning the 2001 Allison Legacy Series, he was NASCAR bound.

1. (tie) Kyle and Kurt Busch (Las Vegas, Nevada). The young drivers who became NASCAR's famous Busch brothers virtually grew up on the bullring short track at Las Vegas Motor Speedway.

Best Things at 16 NASCAR Race Sites (Besides the Raceway)

Most NASCAR fans travel to a race city for the race. When you go to Darlington, South Carolina, the main attraction is the chance to watch a race on one of the most historic race tracks anywhere. Martinsville, Virginia? Ditto. And a trip to Bristol, Tennessee, means some of the most exciting "gladiator style" racing imaginable. But race venues are located in places that offer more than just the race. While no one debates that the race track is the main attraction, here are some favorite next best things at 16 NASCAR race sites.

16. Daytona. One of the world's most famous beaches. Hyde Park Steak House. And the Indiana Jones show at Universal Studios in nearby Orlando.

15. Las Vegas. Potential jackpots. Star sightings. Drive-thru wedding chapels. The fact that what happens here stays here. And Red Rock Canyon.

14. Sonoma. Wine tastings. Ty Caton Vineyards. Bistro Don Giovanni. Heaven for a cork dork.

13. Phoenix. Camelback Mountain. Scenic golf courses. And Sportsman's Fine Wine and Spirits.

12. Watkins Glen. The waterfalls at Watkins Glen State Park.

11. Dover. Crabs at Sambo's. And the Dover Downs Casino next door to the track.

10. Indianapolis. Steaks at St. Elmo Steak House.

9. Texas. Steaks at H3 Ranch at the Stockyards Hotel in Fort Worth.

8. Kansas. Steaks at Hereford House in Kansas City. (Is anyone sensing a theme here?)

7. Richmond. The cigar girls at the Tobacco Company in Shockoe Slip.

6. Michigan. Lack of humidity in August. And Zingerman's Deli in Ann Arbor.

5. Atlanta. The hot dogs at The Varsity, where Kurt Busch worked behind the counter prior to the 2010 race in Atlanta.

4. New Hampshire. Lobster with melted butter at The Weathervane.

3. Charlotte. For drivers who live in Charlotte, the May races mean getting to sleep in their own beds. Also, the dozens of nearby shops, including DEI, Michael Waltrip Racing, Joe Gibbs Racing, etc. And the must-see NASCAR Hall of Fame.

2. Pocono. A heart-shaped Jacuzzi in a honeymoon resort. And the scenery.

1. Darlington. The Raceway Grill, located directly outside the race track gates, just off the back straightaway. Go for the food (the fried chicken and chopped steaks), the history (the grease in the fryer hasn't been changed since Bobby Isaac's day), and the sightings (everyone from NASCAR Sprint Cup Series champions to tire changers).

There are many, many great race broadcasters on the air today. Some of them bring expertise as former drivers or crew chiefs; some are simply great talents who know how to bring racing to the fans in the best possible way. Regarding active broadcasting pros, for the most part, we'll wait and acknowledge them after they retire. Here's just one guy's opinion of the best of the best.

4. Ken Squier. For more than 20 years, the cofounder of the Motor Racing Network called NASCAR races for CBS, and then TBS. It was his voice on the air when the Daytona 500 was broadcast live in 1979. Squier coined the term, the "Great American Race," for the Daytona 500 and became known for expressive phrases, such as "common men doing uncommon things" to refer to drivers and "side over side, end over end" to describe wrecks.

3. Ned Jarrett. After he won the first of his two NASCAR Sprint Cup Series championships in 1961, the painfully shy "Gentleman Ned" decided to polish his speaking skills and signed up for a Dale Carnegie training course in Charlotte. It paid off. He learned to speak to people as a champion and went on to an equally successful career as a broadcaster for CBS and ESPN. In 2011, Jarrett was inducted into the NASCAR Hall of Fame.

2. Benny Parsons. As the 1973 NASCAR Sprint Cup Series champion and winner of the 1975 Daytona 500, Parsons knew what it was like to be a star. But when he became a broadcaster for ESPN in 1989, the first driver to qualify a stock car at more than 200 mph (at Talladega in 1982) took a surprisingly low-key approach. "Everyone can't be stars," Parsons said. "Someone has to sit on the sidewalk and clap as they go by." Fans loved his folksy commentary and his talent for shining the spotlight on his interview subjects rather than himself.

1. Barney Hall. This longtime Motor Racing Network broadcaster once received a compliment from the very understated Bill France Jr., who said, "I like the way you do things. You tell it sort of like it is and you tell it so people can understand what you're talking about." That sums up the appeal of the talented guy with the distinctive delivery who started working in radio in his hometown, Elkin, North Carolina, in 1958.

Coolest Things about the New Car Design

In 2006, NASCAR unveiled a new design template for NASCAR Sprint Cup Series cars. Beginning with the 2007 Bristol Motor Speedway race, all teams were required to run with cars meeting the new design's specs.

At first, some fans didn't like the look of the bigger, boxier design, and drivers weren't comfortable with the handling.

Years later, the car's design remains a work in progress. The safety improvements of the new car speak for themselves. (Just ask Michael McDowell, who flipped his car during a qualifying run at Texas, what he thinks of the new car.) But without question, the new car design has some very cool components.

8. Rear wing. It was replaced by the spoiler after 2010, but for several seasons, the retro rear wing was the new car design's most distinguishing and controversial characteristic.

7. Center seat. The driver's seat sits four inches farther to the right than before, providing more protective space around the person driving the car.

6. Size. The car is bigger than the old design. A larger car punches a bigger and more effective hole in the air. Plus, the larger cockpit (two inches taller and four inches wider) is yet another safety improvement.

5. Windows. The windshield is more upright than in previous car designs, increasing drag. Also, the windows are bigger, which is helpful to drivers climbing in and out of their cars.

4. Foam. The energy-absorbing foam in the side panels and driver's side door is another excellent protective measure.

3. Exhaust. The new car design's exhaust runs through the car's body and exits on the right side, diverting heat away from the driver. Anyone who has ever felt the intense heat inside a race car thinks this is especially cool.

2. Crushability. Although not completely collapsible, the new car design absorbs much more energy and features more crushable materials that further cushion the driver on impact.

1. Claw. Technically, it's a multidimensional body template. But the big, stainless steel claw used by NASCAR inspectors to check the compliance of NASCAR Sprint Cup cars is straight out of a sci-fi flick.

As fast and big and loud as it can be, racing often turns out to be a game of inches. Even the inaugural Daytona 500 in 1959 was literally too close to call, resulting in a photo finish between Johnny Beauchamp and Lee Petty. (Petty was ultimately declared the winner—three days later.) Cale Yarborough clocked dozens of razor-thin wins during his career, none more exciting than in 1984 at Talladega, where he started by winning the Coors Light Pole Award (202.692 mph, a record at the time) and finished by edging Harry Gant for the win.

At Michigan in 1991, Dale Jarrett beat Davey Allison by inches to notch his first-ever NASCAR Sprint Cup Series win.

In 1993, NASCAR switched to electronic timing and scoring, enabling finish times to be calculated to the precise tenth of a second or even hundredth of a second. Here are the closest, down-to-the-wire NASCAR Sprint Cup race finishes since computers started keeping track at the track.

10. Greg Biffle's 2005 win at Homestead-Miami Speedway. He beat Mark Martin by 0.017 seconds.

9. Kevin Harvick's 2010 win at Talladega Superspeedway. He beat Jamie McMurray by 0.011 seconds.

8. Matt Kenseth's 2004 win at Rockingham. He beat Kasey Kahne by 0.010 seconds, tying Dale Earnhardt's 2000 margin of victory.

7. Dale Earnhardt Sr.'s 2000 win at Atlanta Motor Speedway. The Intimidator took the checkered flag by 0.010 seconds over Bobby Labonte.

6. Jimmy Spencer's 1994 win at Daytona International Speedway. Spencer edged out Ernie Irvan by a mere 0.008 seconds.

5. Kevin Harvick's 2001 win at Atlanta Motor Speedway. Harvick, running his third race as Dale Earnhardt Sr.'s replacement in the No. 3 (turned No. 29) car, squeaked by Jeff Gordon with 0.006 seconds to spare. "This one's for Dale," Harvick said.

4. Dale Earnhardt Sr.'s 1993 win at Talladega Superspeedway. Earnhardt beat Ernie Irvan by a margin of 0.005 seconds.

3. Jamie McMurray's 2007 win at Daytona International Raceway. McMurray tied Dale Sr.'s 0.005 seconds mark with his win over Kyle Busch in July 2007.

2. Ricky Craven's 2003 win at Darlington Raceway. Kurt Busch, who had lost his power steering with 10 laps to go, traded paint with Craven down the final straightaway, but lost by 0.002 seconds in the closest finish since the switch to electronic scoring.

1. Jimmie Johnson's 2011 win at Talladega Superspeedway. Johnson tied Craven's record by taking the checkered flag 0.002 seconds ahead of Clint Bowyer, who barely edged Jeff Gordon and Dale Earnhardt Jr. in the thrilling four-wide finish.

So much in NASCAR has evolved during the history of the sport, and that includes the role of the crew chief. In the 1960s, Leonard Wood (of the legendary Wood Brothers Racing) basically defined what it meant to be a crew chief, all the while playing the most hands-on kind of role in the pits. The Waddell Wilsons and Ernie Elliotts of their time were sort of a hybrid between engine builder and crew chief. Robert Yates was owner, engine builder, and somewhat of a crew chief, as well.

Playing the role of everything from wrench turner to administrator, the crew chief is essential to a team's success. He has to be a head coach, strategist, cheerleader, and, at times, even a meteorologist. No easy job.

According to Joe Gibbs, who was one of the hardest-working head coaches in pro football prior to his NASCAR days, an NFL coach has it easy compared to a NASCAR crew chief. As we salute the "Head Wrench," here are some of the best ever.

5. Harry Hyde. Along with his drivers Bobby Isaac, Bobby Allison, Buddy Baker, Neil Bonnett, Dave Marcis, Geoffrey Bodine, and Tim Richmond, Hyde collected 56 NASCAR Sprint Cup wins and took one NASCAR Sprint Cup championship (with Isaac). But Hyde may be best remembered for his technical innovations and the record-setting performances of his cars and drivers, including Isaac's record run of 201.104 mph at Talladega in 1970, a mark that stood until Cale Yarborough broke it in 1983.

4. Andy Petree. As the two-time NASCAR Sprint Cup Series championship crew chief for Dale Earnhardt Sr., Petree, who got his big break as a tire changer for championship-winner Darrell Waltrip, has a permanent place in NASCAR's history books.

3. Ray Evernham. Three championships during his six years as Jeff Gordon's crew chief position mean that Evernham is one of the best ever. He was a pioneer during an evolving era in which crew chiefs oversaw a fleet of cars, instead of just two or three, and prepared them to run on varying courses from restrictor-plate tracks to short tracks.

2. Chad Knaus. On Knaus's watch, Jimmie Johnson has won five consecutive championships. And counting.

1. Dale Inman. Although Inman graciously denies that he should be named the best (he picks Leonard Wood as the top pit boss of all time), statistics don't lie. Inman spent almost three decades as Richard Petty's crew chief, and together they won seven NASCAR Sprint Cup championships. In 1984, he notched another championship with Terry Labonte. Besides gaining a bucket of wins, Inman established his legacy by how he redefined the duties of crew chief to include race preparation and driver-pit communication.

Every driver wants to win at Daytona. Tony Stewart once said he would do anything to win this race, including sliding upside down across the finish line. As the first and most prestigious race of the NASCAR Sprint Cup Series season, the Daytona 500 has provided plenty of memorable moments over the years—some heartbreakers, some spectacular, some literally too close to call. Racing is never dull at Daytona. From Petty to Bayne, here are some of the races we'll never forget.

11. Derrike Cope's Bolt from the Blue (1990). Dale Earnhardt Sr. led 155 laps and, at one point, almost lapped the field. Then, after cutting a tire on the last lap, Earnhardt was out and newcomer Derrike Cope, making only his third Daytona 500 start, bested Terry Labonte to take the checkered flag.

10. Waltrip's Lucky 17 (1989). One of the most famous narratives in racing is Dale Earnhardt Sr.'s long path to winning the Daytona 500. But the path of Darrell Waltrip, who failed to win the Daytona 500 in his first 16 attempts, was nearly as long. Then in 1989, while driving the No. 17 car during his 17th attempt, Waltrip finally made it to Victory Lane.

9. Allison-Allison One-Two Finish (1988). At age 50, Bobby Allison became the oldest winner in Daytona 500 history. If that wasn't enough for the record books, Allison's son, Davey, finished second, marking the only time in history a father and son have finished one-two in the Great American Race.

8. King's Seventh Win (1981). When Richard Petty won the Daytona 500 in 1981, he became the only driver to win the Great American Race seven times. When he marked his sixth win in 1979, no other driver had won at Daytona more than twice. It's good to be the King.

7. Harvick Edges Martin (2007). In the closest Daytona 500 finish since the introduction of electronic scoring, Kevin Harvick edged Mark Martin by 0.02 seconds to clinch the victory.

6. Junior's Win (2004). Dale Earnhardt Jr. led the first lap and led when it counted for a win that put him and his late father in the company of the only other two father-son Daytona 500 winners—the Pettys and the Allisons.

5. Petty–Pearson Finish (1976). Fans were used to seeing rivals Richard Petty and David Pearson battle for the checkered flag. Coming into the 1976 season, the duo had 57 one-two finishes. In the Bicentennial Daytona 500, Petty and Pearson swapped the lead four times during the final lap and tangled in the fourth turn. Following the wreck, Pearson managed to straighten out his car and sputter across the finish line to win the race.

4. Infield Rumble (1979). Richard Petty won the race, which was broadcast live on CBS with incredible Nielsen ratings. But that's not what we remember. People still talk about the final-lap crash that led to a rumble in the infield, where Cale Yarborough, Donnie Allison, and Bobby Allison climbed out of their cars and came to blows.

3. Cinderella Story (2011). On the day after his 20th birthday and in just his second NASCAR Sprint Cup career start, Trevor Bayne won the Daytona 500 for one of the greatest upset victories in NASCAR history.

2. Earnhardt Wins (1998). It was NASCAR's 50th anniversary year and after 20 years of trying, the champion who had won just about everything else and everywhere else finally won the race that kept eluding him. In Victory Lane, his joy was contagious, "Daytona is ours!" Dale Earnhardt Sr. shouted. "We won it, we won it, we won it!"

1. The First Great American Race (1959). The inaugural Daytona 500 was memorable beyond the fact that it was the first. Johnny Beauchamp and Lee Petty finished nose-to-nose, with Beauchamp flagged the winner. But after officials examined film and photos for three days, Lee Petty was declared the winner. And history was made.

When it's your job to talk about NASCAR, the least you can do is correctly pronounce the names of the principals. Sometimes that's easier said than done. Or not so easier said than done. Here's how we keep the toughest, most tongue-twisting names straight.

9. AJ Allmendinger. Jimmy Spencer just skips it and calls him, "AJ Pull My Finger." Best to linger over the initials and say the last name slowly.

8. Alan Gustafson. In this case, "s" before "f."

7. Aric Almirola. Hint: Amarillo is a city in Texas. Almirola drives race cars.

6. Rick Hendrick. People often say "Hendricks." Just remember, Hendrix played guitar. Hendrick owns race cars.

5. Patrick Carpentier. Not the handyman. But a driver named Carpentier.

4. Parker Kligerman. Not "Kling." Kligg . . .

3. Travis Kvapil. The "v" is pronounced as a "w."

2. Tad Geschickter. There is no helpful hint.

1. Marcos Ambrose. Almost everyone calls him "Marcose" Ambrose at least once. We try really hard not to.

NASCAR is really just one gigantic family. No other sport features the same competitors at every venue for every event during a season that lasts 10 months a year. So drivers, crews, and their families get to know each other very well. It's a traveling show, and drivers tend to bring their families along when they go racing. Especially when they're just starting out.

Early in Ned Jarrett's career, he would put the whole clan in the family car, which was also his race car, and drive to the track. If he wrecked the car during a race, he had to ask around and arrange for a lift home for the entire family. All the way back to North Carolina.

ARCA champion Frank Kimmel often talks about his dad driving through the night with his family to get home following Sunday races. His mom would stick a wet rag in a cooler full of cold water and put it on his father's face so he didn't fall asleep at the wheel. That's racing.

Although there have been many great families with fathers and sons, and sisters and brothers involved in the sport, a handful of families have gone beyond making NASCAR a family affair. They have established racing dynasties.

5. The Jarretts. Ned and Dale Jarrett made up only the second father-son NASCAR Sprint Cup Series champion duo. Both had tremendous racing careers (as of 2011, Ned is tied for No. 11 and Dale is No. 21 on the all-time wins list). And even more incredibly, they managed to do it while being nice to people. (Ned even earned a nice guy nickname, "Gentleman Ned.") When Dale's son, Jason, competed in the NASCAR Nationwide Series, the Jarretts became a three generation racing clan.

4. The Allisons. The only family to notch more NASCAR Sprint Cup wins than the Allisons is the Pettys. Between brothers Bobby and Donnie, and Bobby's son, Davey, the Allisons stood in Victory Lane 113 times in a total of 1,151 races. Sadly, though, the trio that formed the core of the famed "Alabama Gang" had its share of tragedy, as well as triumph. In 1993, Davey died in a helicopter crash just five years after his brother, Clifford, died as a result of an on-track crash. In 2011, Bobby was inducted into the NASCAR Hall of Fame.

3. The Earnhardts. Ralph Earnhardt drove race cars for 23 years and was known for his mastery of North Carolina short tracks. During his 51 NASCAR Sprint Cup race starts, he posted 16 top 10 finishes. His son, Dale Earnhardt Sr., became NASCAR's Intimidator, winning seven NASCAR Sprint Cup championships and 76 races before he died following a last-lap accident at the 2001 Daytona 500.

Dale Sr.'s youngest son, Dale Jr., is a NASCAR Sprint Cup competitor and eight-time winner of NASCAR's Most Popular Driver Award. Dale Sr.'s oldest son, Kerry, competed in various stock car series and made seven NASCAR Sprint Cup starts before retiring in 2009. Kerry's son Jeffrey began racing for DEI in 2007.

2. The Pettys. First came Lee Petty, a stock car racing pioneer who won the inaugural Daytona 500 in 1959. He passed the torch to his son, Richard, who won his first championship in 1964, the same year Lee retired. Richard went on to become NASCAR's King, logging seven championships and 200 victories during the next two decades.

In 1979, Richard's son, Kyle, officially joined the family business, claiming his first NASCAR Sprint Cup victory in 1986 and notching his best two seasons in 1992 and 1993, finishing fifth in the final points standings both years. Kyle went on to serve as CEO of Petty Enterprises, and then moved into a successful broadcasting career. Perhaps most admirably, in 2004, Kyle and his wife, Pattie, opened Victory Junction, a camp for seriously ill children established in the memory of their son, Adam, who died following an on-track accident in 2000.

1. The Frances. Without this family, there would literally be no NASCAR. It all began when a former mechanic and gas station owner, William H.G. "Big Bill" France, formed the National Association of Stock Car Racing in 1948. He built the grandest race tracks (at Daytona and Talladega), established a motorsports empire, and passed the reigns to his son Bill Jr. in 1972.

As CEO and Chairman of the Board, Bill Jr. oversaw the explosive national growth of the sport and all the sponsorships, TV contracts, and superstars that came with it.

In 2003, Bill Jr.'s son, Brian France, took over as Chairman of the Board and CEO of NASCAR. NASCAR remains a France family enterprise: Bill Jr.'s brother, Jim, serves as vice chairman and executive vice president/assistant secretary; Brian's sister, Lesa Kennedy, serves as vice chairwoman, executive vice president/assistant treasurer, as well as the CEO of the International Speedway Corporation (ISC), which was formed by her grandfather; Bill Jr.'s wife, Betty Jane, has long served as NASCAR assistant secretary and is also the chairwoman and founder of The NASCAR Foundation.

In 2010, both Bill France Sr. and Bill France Jr. were NASCAR Hall of Fame Inaugural Inductees.

There are more bold-faced names who call themselves race fans than you could count. Some grew up going to NASCAR tracks. Some learned to love stock car racing after attending an event for the first time. It's easy to understand why the following famous folks caught the NASCAR bug.

18. Clarence Thomas. The Supreme Court justice has attended dozens of races, which he travels to in his motor home. He knows his stuff, too; Thomas can name all the active drivers, along with their hometowns and points standings.

17. Kevin Costner. A regular at races, the actor even wrote a song, "Backyard," about guys who build and fix race cars. Costner served as the 2009 spokesperson for The NASCAR Foundation and narrated the NASCAR documentary, *The Ride of Their Lives*.

16. Hulk Hogan. An enormous Richard Petty fan, the outsized personality and pro wrestling legend began life as Terry Gene Bollea, growing up in Tampa and watching races.

15. Tom Cruise. The actor starred in the movie, *Days of Thunder*, raced with Paul Newman for fun, and drove in the Sports Car Club of America (SCCA) Show-room Stock Series with Rick Hendrick. He still attends many races, often with his son, Connor.

14. Mario Batali. The celebrity chef, who wrote the cookbook, *Mario Tailgates NASCAR Style*, has been spotted at more than 50 NASCAR races.

13. Rachel Ray. The talk-show host and entrepreneur was introduced to NASCAR by her friend and fellow TV chef Mario Batali.

12. Guy Fieri. The Food Network star and host of the TV game show, *Minute to Win It*, served as grand marshal at Infineon Raceway in 2008 and still hits the race track grandstands whenever possible. This self-described "car guy" even sponsored a car for Tommy Baldwin Racing at the 2009 Brickyard 400.

11. George Martin. The former New York Giants lineman became a NASCAR fan after attending a race at Phoenix in 2008 as part of his walk from New York to San Diego (A Journey for 9/11) to raise money for first responders affected by the 2001 terrorist attacks.

10. Angie Harmon. Arguably our all-time favorite guest in *Victory Lane*, Harmon and her husband, former New York Giants defensive back, Jason Sehorn, are often spotted at NASCAR events. Harmon's recurring on-track roles include honorary starter and pace car driver.

9. Will Ferrell. How could the guy who ran up the banking at Charlotte Motor Speedway in his underwear for the movie, *Talladega Nights: The Ballad of Ricky Bobby*, not be a fan? FYI, he still has the firesuit he wore in the flick.

8. Kevin James. A repeat grand marshal, the actor can't seem to stay away from the track.

7. Ronald Reagan. The first sitting U.S. president to attend a NASCAR race (at Daytona in 1984), Reagan actually gave the command, "Gentlemen, start your engines" from aboard Air Force One. Who wouldn't be a fan after watching Richard Petty score his 200th win?

6. Aerosmith. The members of Aerosmith count themselves as die-hard race fans. A live version of their hit "Back in the Saddle"—complete with new, race-themed lyrics—was played during many race telecasts in 2007. In 1999, Kenny Wallace drove an Aerosmith-sponsored Chevrolet.

5. Jackie Joyner-Kersee. The Olympic track-and-field champion was one of the fastest women in the world and took her love for speed to the track when she and husband, Bob Kersee, bought a NASCAR racing team, JKR Motorsports.

4. Michael Mauldin. NASCAR is in the blood for Mauldin, a hip-hop producer and the first African American president of Columbia Records. His father, Lightning, was a moonshine driver and Mauldin grew up in North Carolina's Smoky Mountains loving cars.

3. (tie) Troy Aikman and Roger Staubach. These multiple Super Bowl winners and Hall of Fame quarterbacks for the Dallas Cowboys turned their love of the track into a race team, Hall of Fame Racing, which had its best season with driver Tony Raines in 2007.

2. Randy Moss. The NFL wide receiver is a race fan turned team owner of Randy Moss Motorsports, which fields trucks in the NASCAR Camping World Truck Series.

1. Brian Williams. The *NBC Nightly News* anchor is an enthusiastic race fan with a concise explanation for his passion: "It's plain and simple: I like speed. Just give me the first turn at Talladega, when they come around at speed on the second lap. I defy you to replicate that feeling anywhere else in life."

Williams honors his favorite driver, Dale Earnhardt Sr., by carrying No. 3 stickers with him everywhere he goes and leaving them behind on rental cars or even in exotic places, such as one of Saddam Hussein's former palaces in Iraq.

From the tri-ovals to the D-shaped tracks and road courses, every NASCAR Sprint Cup Series track has a clear-cut pavement personality. Certain characteristics, such as steep banking or long straightaways, not only define what a track looks like, but pretty much determine what fans can expect to happen on race day. Here is some track-by-track trivia for inquiring race fans.

23. Atlanta Motor Speedway (first NASCAR Sprint Cup race: 1960; distance: 1.54 miles).

Fireball Roberts won the first race on a rainy, muddy day at Atlanta Motor Speedway back in 1960. Years later in 2005, a deadly tornado wreaked havoc on the track, but damage to scoring pylons and other track components were repaired in time for the scheduled race that year.

22. Auto Club Speedway (first NASCAR Sprint Cup race: 1997; distance: 2.0 miles).

The track was built in 1996 on the site of the former Kaiser Steel Mill. In 2004, lights were added at the speedway, which is often featured in TV shows, commercials, and movies, including *Charlie's Angels* (2000) and *Herbie: Fully Loaded* (2004). In 2007, Morgan Freeman and Jack Nicholson used the track to film a scene in which they race a vintage Shelby Mustang and Dodge Challenger in *The Bucket List*.

21. Bristol Motor Speedway (first NASCAR Sprint Cup race: 1961; distance: 0.533 mile).

It's been said that after racing at Bristol, a driver either brings home the trophy or brings home his steering wheel. Bristol has some of the NASCAR circuit's steepest banking (up to 30 degrees), which causes drivers to inevitably mix it up in races. Three Bristol races have featured 20 cautions. Twelve-time winner Darrell Waltrip has won here the most.

20. Charlotte Motor Speedway (first NASCAR Sprint Cup race: 1960; distance: 1.5 miles).

Considered many NASCAR drivers' home track, Charlotte Motor Speedway is the site of the annual NASCAR Sprint All-Star Race and is the only track to host 600-mile races. Seven drivers have won Charlotte's back-to-back NASCAR Sprint All-Star Race and Coca-Cola 600 in the same season—Darrell Waltrip (1985), Davey Allison (1991), Dale Earnhardt Sr. (1993), Jeff Gordon (1997), Jimmie Johnson (2003), Kasey Kahne (2008), and Kurt Busch (2010).

19. Chicagoland Speedway (first NASCAR Sprint Cup race: 2001; distance: 1.5 miles). Jimmie Johnson set the track qualifying record of 188.147 mph in 2005, but Chicago—the tri-oval with the distinctive curve in the backstretch—remains one of only five tracks where Johnson has not won a race.

18. Darlington Raceway (first NASCAR Sprint Cup race: 1950; distance: 1.366 miles). Nicknamed the "Lady in Black" because drivers are known to brush the white retaining wall with their tires and turn it black, Darlington was initially built on a cotton and peanut field. The track took on its egg-like shape because construction crews had to build around a minnow farm that the former landowner refused to move.

17. Daytona International Speedway (first NASCAR Sprint Cup race: 1959; distance: 2.5 miles). Richard Petty has won most often (10 times) in the NASCAR Sprint Cup points events at this storied track that is home to the Daytona 500. The track got a facelift in 2011, the same year that a Florida Senate Committee voted down a bill that would have allowed a columbarium (a building that houses urns) to be built on-site to house the cremated ashes of deceased racing fans.

16. Dover International Speedway (first NASCAR Sprint Cup race: 1969; distance: 1.0 mile). The surfaces of most modern tracks consist of asphalt, but five-time NASCAR Sprint Cup champion Jimmie Johnson's favorite track is made of concrete, which makes it exceptionally mean to cars (hence its "Monster Mile" nickname).

15. Homestead-Miami Speedway (first NASCAR Sprint Cup race: 1999; distance: 1.5 miles). Originally a rectangular oval that required four lakes to be dug for its construction, Homestead was reconfigured to its current oval shape in 1997 (steeper banking was eventually added). Two years later, NASCAR Sprint Cup races were annual events in South Florida.

14. Indianapolis Motor Speedway (first NASCAR Sprint Cup race: 1994; distance: 2.5 miles). This famed Indy 500 host track, also known as the Brickyard, was originally paved with bricks that still line the yard of bricks at the start/finish line.

13. Infineon Raceway (first NASCAR Sprint Cup race: 1989; distance: 1.99 miles). Each nearly two-mile lap contains 12 turns, providing drivers with more opportunities to turn right than on any other race track. Ricky Rudd won the first-ever NASCAR race at this road-course track.

12. Kansas Speedway (first NASCAR Sprint Cup race: 2001; distance: 1.5 miles). This track is one of several tracks that host two events per season. In 2011, the seats in the grandstands were expanded by two inches. No word on whether corn dog consumption had anything to do with this.

11. Kentucky Speedway (first NASCAR Sprint Cup race: 2011; distance: 1.5 miles). NASCAR's newest track was awarded a race date from Atlanta Motor Speedway. During the track's inaugural NASCAR Sprint Cup race in July 2011, Kyle Busch outlasted David Reutimann by 0.179 seconds.

10. Las Vegas Motor Speedway (first NASCAR Sprint Cup race: 1998; distance: 1.5 miles). The race at the Sin City track is always unique—from the Vegas strip parade of NASCAR haulers (the trucks that carry a team's race car and equipment to the track), to its grand marshals, such as Wayne Newton and Kim Kardashian.

9. Martinsville Speedway (first NASCAR Sprint Cup race: 1949; distance: 0.526 mile). If its walls could talk. . . . The track known as the "Paperclip" is the shortest, as well as the oldest, continually operating NASCAR track. Following the first-ever race at Martinsville, track owner Clay Earles said, "It was the dustiest place I've ever seen. When the race started, it looked like someone had dropped a bomb."

8. Michigan International Speedway (first NASCAR Sprint Cup race: 1969; distance: 2.0 miles). Its long straightaways and wide turns make Michigan one of NASCAR's fastest tracks.

7. New Hampshire Motor Speedway (first NASCAR Sprint Cup race: 1993; distance: 1.058 miles). The "Magic Mile" was the site of the first single day sporting event in New England (the July 2000 NASCAR Sprint Cup race) to draw more than 100,000 fans.

6. Phoenix International Raceway (first NASCAR Sprint Cup race: 1988; distance: 1.0 mile). Before every race at Phoenix, which was repaved and reconfigured in 2011, crews clear approximately 800 rattlesnakes off Rattlesnake Hill, an area where fans sit and watch the race. Which begs the question, did they get them all?

5. Pocono Raceway (first NASCAR Sprint Cup race: 1974; distance: 2.5 miles). Turn One at Pocono, the only triangle-shaped NASCAR track, was modeled after a turn at the now-defunct Trenton Speedway. Turn Two is a nod to Indianapolis Motor Speedway and Turn Three is reminiscent of the Milwaukee Mile.

4. Richmond International Raceway (first NASCAR Sprint Cup race: 1953; distance: .75 mile). Originally a half-mile oval, Richmond was later reconfigured to its current three-quarter-mile length. Since lights were installed in the early 1990s, night races have been the norm at what some call a perfect track.

3. Talladega Superspeedway (first NASCAR Sprint Cup race: 1969; distance: 2.66 miles). The Intimidator, Dale Earnhardt Sr., was Talladega's dominator; he posted 10 NASCAR Sprint Cup wins at NASCAR's largest superspeedway, which was built on unpretentious soybean farm acreage located next to several abandoned airport runways.

2. Texas Motor Speedway (first NASCAR Sprint Cup race: 1997; distance: 1.5 miles). In 2000, Dale Jr. won his first NASCAR Sprint Cup race at this Fort Worth track. In 2011, NASA astronaut Doug Hurley was presented with a Texas Motor Speedway flag to carry with him on the final space shuttle mission.

1. Watkins Glen International (first NASCAR Sprint Cup race: 1957, distance: 2.45 miles). Buck Baker won the first NASCAR Sprint Cup race at this seven-turn road course in 1957. In 1992, reconstruction on the inner loop and back straightaway was completed, resulting in a safer track and better views for the fans.

NASCAR drivers' uniforms are among the most distinctive in all of sports. When you see the helmet and multicolored firesuit splashed with logos of every make and stripe, there is no mistaking what the guy or girl wearing it does for a living.

It didn't used to be that way. During NASCAR's formative years, competitors actually drove in jeans and regular shoes. (There was also a NASCAR series solely for convertibles, but that's another story.) They wore undershirts or T-shirts they brought from home, usually plain white ones or a freebie emblazoned with the logo of an auto parts company.

Until the early 1970s, drivers wore half-helmets and goggles, often purchased at their hometown Army Navy surplus store.

Today, most speedways require competitors to wear full-faced helmets, along with flame-resistant clothing, gloves, underwear, and shoes. And regarding firesuits, the more colorful, the better.

It's a challenge to stand out in this crowd. But here is some garb (and a few distinguishing characteristics) that helped NASCAR stars do just that.

20. Richie Panch's helmet. The full-faced helmet he wore in 1973 is believed to be the first custom-painted helmet worn in NASCAR's premier series.

19. Tiny Lund's driver uniform. In the early 1970s, Lund squeezed his 300-plus-pound frame into a suit made of a whole lot of fireproof fabric.

18. Tim Richmond's snakeskin cowboy boots. As flamboyant as the driver who wore them.

17. Glen Wood's pit crew shirt. In the mid-1960s, the fastest team in the pits was also the best-dressed in their coordinated uniforms.

16. Junior Johnson's overalls. Next to in his firesuit, the NASCAR Hall of Fame Inaugural Inductee is most comfortable—and recognizable—in a denim pair of coveralls.

15. Rick Hendrick's aviator jacket. He designed it himself.

14. Dave Marcis's wing tips. One of the last drivers to wear an open-faced helmet, Marcis also set himself apart by wearing wing-tip shoes.

13. Raymond Parks's hat and tie. A team owner, NASCAR founding member, and a Southern gentleman, Parks always wore dapper hats, tailored suits, and elegant ties to the track from the 1930s until he passed away in 2010.

12. Kyle Busch's sunglasses. People try to get Kyle's goat by saying he wears his wife's sunglasses.

11. Ned Jarrett's custom driving suit. For his final season of 1966, Gentleman Ned had a special turquoise suit made with his name and No. 11 embroidered on it in white.

10. Donnie Allison's driving shoes. In the early 1960s, Allison wore shoes with metal studs to protect his feet from the boiling hot transmission tunnel near his car's gas pedal area.

9. Tony Stewart's tattoo. Although he won't show it or divulge its exact location, Smoke evidently has a tattoo based on the design of his helmet.

8. Kyle Petty's No. 45 cap. KP wears this cap with a black band through the No. 45 to honor his son Adam, who died in 2000 as a result of an accident during a practice run at New Hampshire Motor Speedway.

7. Smokey Yunick's uniform. The renowned mechanic, car builder, and car owner was rarely seen without his trademark white uniform, battered boots, cowboy hat, and signature cigar or corncob pipe.

6. Jeff Gordon's helmet, circa 1995. Gordon's brightly colored helmet matched his car and led to his crew being called the "Rainbow Warriors."

5. DeLana Harvick's firesuit. Driver Kevin Harvick's wife, DeLana, started wearing a firesuit while watching races from the pit box in the early 2000s. She says it was a safety thing. Her firesuit became famous when her husband tangled with Joey Logano at Pocono in 2010 and Logano said, "His wife wears the firesuit in the family and tells him what to do. It's probably not his fault."

4. Fonty Flock's Bermuda shorts. This was one way to stay cool a decade or two before ventilation systems.

3. Jack Roush's straw hat. As co-owner and CEO of Roush Fenway Racing, Roush wears many hats. But most identify the man known as the "Cat in the Hat" with his trademark straw fedora.

2. Darrell Waltrip's chrome firesuit. DW not only drove a chrome-plated race car, he made a fashion statement by wearing a chrome helmet and matching silver firesuit.

1. Richard Petty's feathered Charlie 1 Horse Stetson, signature belt buckle, and cowboy boots. This combination absolutely screams, "The King is here!"

Best Golf Courses Close to the Track

Just because someone can successfully drive a race car doesn't mean he can successfully drive a golf ball down the fairway. Even so, between celebrity golf tournaments and playing a few rounds on days off, golf is a constant in the lives of many people who drive race cars for a living. Here are a few courses where you just might spot a driver wielding a driver.

5. Loudon Country Club, Loudon, New Hampshire. Designed by William Leombruno, this 18-hole course sits right on Route 106, just down the road from the New Hampshire Motor Speedway. It features 6,008 yards of golf from its back tees, a total par of 70, a rating of 69.2, and a slope rating of 123.

4. Rocky River Golf Club, Concord, North Carolina. Located right on Bruton Smith Boulevard in Concord, this 18-hole course is close enough to the Charlotte Motor Speedway to hear the revving of the engines, but you'll feel miles away. Its meticulously manicured layout and rolling hills help rank it in North Carolina's top 100.

3. Joliet Country Club, Joliet, Illinois. Designed by Scotland's Tom Bendelow in the early 1900s, this is a hilly, well-maintained course with tight fairways and small, fast greens. According to thegolfcourses.net, the signature hole is No. 16, a 345-yard par 4 from an elevated tee, down a small fairway with a creek running through its center. The course sits close enough to Chicagoland Speedway to let you play a round on it in the morning while allowing you to still catch a late afternoon or evening race.

2. Golf Club of Estrella, Goodyear, Arizona. Phoenix and other nearby Arizona cities and towns are home to dozens of great golf courses. (They have the space.) Drivers and TV crew guys who answered a crack poll picked the 18-hole, par-72 championship Golf Club of Estrella as a favorite. It's the first daily fee course designed by Jack Nicklaus II, and its views of the Sierra Estrella Mountains and the desert terrain are fantastic. It's public, but feels like an exclusive private course.

1. Brickyard Crossing at Indianapolis. Talk about playing through. Four holes of this course sit inside the Brickyard oval and the other 14 holes are adjacent to the track's backstretch. Designed by noted golf course designer and architect Pete Dye, Brickyard Crossing was ranked in the top 100 courses in the country by *Golf Digest* and *Golf Week*, and is one of just a few courses to host PGA, LPGA, and Champions Tour Events.

For Starters (and Grand Marshals)

The most famous four words in racing are, "Gentlemen, start your engines."

Most often, the grand marshal is the lucky person who gets to say these words and officially start the race.

The tradition of big racing events bringing in a special guest to host a parade, wave the green flag, or give the start command goes way back to the 1930s, when the Indy 500 featured luminaries—such as former heavyweight boxing champ Gene Tunney, and pioneering female aviators Amelia Earhart and Jackie Cochran—as "honorary referees."

According to Charlotte Motor Speedway President Humpy Wheeler, the original grand marshals were referred to as "honorary starters." Sometimes the honoree didn't start the race but just drove the pace car, as was the case with *CBS News* anchor Walter Cronkite at Daytona in 1965. (Although, there's a guy who should definitely have said the words.)

Over the years, grand marshals and/or starters have included politicians, sitting presidents, former NASCAR champions, moms of drivers, sports stars, movie stars, and plenty of corporate folks chosen by sponsors.

Mostly, grand marshals stick to the script, although the morning radio hosts, John Boy and Billy, deserve a shout out for improvisation when, at the former North Wilkesboro Speedway, they said, "Gentlemen—and Jimmy Spencer—start your engines."

Daytona International Speedway has drawn the most prestigious grand marshals over the years, including the first sitting U.S. president to attend a race, Ronald Reagan, who gave the "Gentlemen, start your engines" command prior to Richard Petty's 200th win at the 1984 Firecracker 400. There have been dozens of others, though. Here are some standouts (listed chronologically).

Daytona 500 Grand Marshals

9. George C. Wallace (1973). Alabama governor and presidential candidate.

8. Clarence Thomas (1999). Supreme Court justice.

7. John Travolta (2003). TV and film actor (*Pulp Fiction*, *Saturday Night Fever*).

6. George W. Bush (2004). U.S. president.

5. Matthew McConaughey (2005). Film actor (*A Time to Kill*, *Failure to Launch*).

4. James Caan (2006). Film and TV actor (*The Godfather*, *Las Vegas*).

3. Nicolas Cage (2007). Academy Award-winning film actor (*Leaving Las Vegas*, *Raising Arizona*).

2. Twenty-four Daytona 500 Champions (2008).

1. Josh Duhamel, Rosie Huntington-Whitely and Michael Bay (2011), actors and director (*Transformers: Dark of the Moon*).

Daytona 500 Honorary Starters

10. Charlie Rich (1975). Grammy-winning country music singer.

9. James Michener (1978). Author of dozens of best-selling books and winner of the 1977 Presidential Medal of Freedom.

8. Troy Aikman (1994). Quarterback of then-reigning NFL Super Bowl champion Dallas Cowboys who went on to claim three Super Bowl rings and a Hall of Fame spot.

7. Dan Marino (1998). Pro Football Hall of Fame quarterback and network broadcaster.

6. Brett Favre (1999). Super Bowl winner who holds multiple career records for Pro Football quarterbacks.

5. Terry Bradshaw (2001). Three-time Super Bowl champion, Pro Football Hall of Fame quarterback, and network broadcaster.

4. Angie Harmon (2002). Model and TV actress (*Law and Order*, *Baywatch Nights*).

3. Mariah Carey (2003). Five-time Grammy-winning singer.

2. Whoopi Goldberg (2004). Comedian, TV host (*The View*), and Oscar-winning actress (*Ghost*).

1. Ashton Kutcher (2005). TV and film actor (*That '70s Show*; *Dude, Where's My Car?*).

Grand Marshals for Daytona's July Race
3. Britney Spears (2001). Actress and Grammy-winning singer.

2. Jessica Simpson (2002). Actress and singer.

1. Kevin James (2007). TV and film actor (*King of Queens*, *Paul Blart: Mall Cop*).

From Other Tracks
21. Cal Ripken Jr., Grand Marshal and Honorary Starter (Dover International Speedway, 2001). World Series winner and Baseball Hall of Famer who holds the record for playing in the most consecutive games.

20. Joe Montana, Co-Grand Marshal (Kansas Speedway, 2002). Four-time Super Bowl winner and Pro Football Hall of Fame quarterback.

19. Reggie Jackson, Co-Grand Marshal (Kansas Speedway, 2002). Five-time World Series winner and Baseball Hall of Famer.

18. Representatives from the Army, Navy, Air Force, Marine Corps, and Coast Guard (Bristol Motor Speedway, 2002).

17. Jim Kelly, Grand Marshal (Talladega Superspeedway, 2003). Pro Football Hall of Fame quarterback.

16. Mark Sanford, Grand Marshal (Darlington Raceway, 2003). South Carolina governor. (Note: This was long before Sanford resigned over scandals).

15. Pamela Anderson, Grand Marshal (Charlotte Motor Speedway, 2005). Model and actress (*Baywatch*).

14. Jackie Joyner-Kersee, Co-Grand Marshal (Kansas Speedway, 2006). Heptathlete and long jumper who won three Olympic gold medals.

13. George Lopez, Co-Grand Marshal (Kansas Speedway, 2006). Comedian.

12. Will Ferrell, Grand Marshal (Chicagoland Speedway and Talledega Superspeedway, 2006). TV and film actor (*Saturday Night Live*, *Talladega Nights: The Ballad of Ricky Bobby*).

11. Rob Schneider, Co-Grand Marshal (Atlanta Motor Speedway, 2006). Film and TV actor.

10. David Spade, Co-Grand Marshal (Atlanta Motor Speedway, 2006). Film and TV actor.

9. Jon Heder, Co-Grand Marshal (Atlanta Motor Speedway, 2006). Film and TV actor.

8. Drivers' moms (Darlington Raceway, 2006). At Darlington, they invite a group of moms ("Sons and Gentlemen, start your engines!") to host the Saturday Mother's Day weekend race. The mom grand marshals have included:

Carol Bickford (Jeff Gordon); Ramona Vickers (Brian Vickers); Becky Sorenson (Reed Sorenson); Martha Labonte (Terry and Bobby Labonte); Nancy Sterling (Carl Edwards); Gaye Busch (Kurt and Kyle Busch); Diane Newman (Ryan Newman); Mary Lou Hamlin (Denny Hamlin); Linda Truex (Martin Truex Jr.); Bell Sadler (Hermie and Elliott Sadler); Margaret Waltrip (Michael Waltrip); Meredith Bowman (Jeff Burton); Jana Bowyer (Clint Bowyer); Joan Wimmer (Scott Wimmer); Susie Nolff (Scott Riggs); and Pam Boas (Tony Stewart).

7. Michael Jordan, Grand Marshal (Charlotte Motor Speedway, 2007).
Six-time NBA champion and Hall of Famer.

6. Howie Long, Grand Marshal (Texas Motor Speedway, 2009). Super
Bowl winner, Pro Football Hall of Famer, and network broadcaster.

5. Ken Stabler, Grand Marshal (Infineon Raceway, 2009). Super Bowl
champion quarterback.

4. Bill Dance, Co-Grand Marshal (Atlanta Motor Speedway, 2003). TV
fishing show host (*Bill Dance Outdoors*).

**3. Adam Sandler, Co-Grand Marshal (Michigan International Speed-
way, 2010).** Along with fellow actor/comedian Kevin James, Sandler teamed up for
probably the longest "Gentlemen, start your engines" in history.

**2. Stone Cold Steve Austin, Grand Marshal (Bristol Motor Speedway,
2010).** Pro wrestling superstar.

**1. Wayne Newton, Grand Marshal (Las Vegas Motor Speedway, on
multiple occasions).** Actor and singer known as Mr. Las Vegas.

Best All-Time Grand Marshal
**Matthew Hansen, Grand Marshal (Richmond International Raceway,
2011).** The NASCAR Sprint Cup Series race, the Matthew and Daniel Hansen 400,
was named for the identical twin Hansen brothers, military heroes who served together in the Marines. Daniel Hansen was killed in action in Afghanistan in 2009; his
brother, Matthew, served as grand marshal in his honor.

TV broadcasters are notoriously fussy about their hair. At SPEED, we kid with former crew chief turned FOX Sports racing analyst Larry McReynolds that his hair spray usage may single-handedly deplete the ozone layer. We also give former crew chief turned FOX broadcaster Jeff Hammond a hard time about his hair, which always looks good and perfectly complements his tan (the running joke is that Jeff spends half his time in the tanning booth and the other half in the broadcast booth). And Rutledge Wood. Need we say more?

Being that NASCAR drivers wear helmets a lot of the time, you wouldn't think that fans would notice their hair. But they do. When Jeff Gordon's wife brushed his hair out of his face while the national anthem was being played prior to the 2008 Bud Shootout, fans literally were all a-Twitter. And if a guy grows a beard—think Tony Stewart, Jimmie Johnson, or Dale Jr.—fans will definitely have something to say about it.

Some drivers deliberately try to make statements with their hair. Some make statements without really trying to. Here are some of the hairiest situations NASCAR has seen.

13. Denny Hamlin's crew shaving their heads. Members of Hamlin's pit crew said they would shave their heads if they won the 2011 NASCAR Sprint Pit Crew Challenge Presented by Craftsman. They won and they did shave their heads. On live TV. The look on the rear tire changer's face before the razor came out was priceless.

12. Kevin Harvick's crew growing facial hair. In 2011, as part of Anheuser Busch's Grow One Campaign to promote saving water, Harvick and crew stopped shaving for a few weeks. Did this have anything to do with Harvick's winning streak during this period?

11. Elliott Sadler's annual beard. It's not for looks. Not for superstition. Sadler says he grows his beard for deer hunting season.

10. AJ Allmendinger's hair. For years, Allmendinger has vowed to bring sexy back to racing. If sexy means hair gel and volumizing tonic, then AJ's work is done.

9. Jason Leffler's mohawk (or faux hawk). Perfect for a driver sponsored by Great Clips.

8. Kyle Petty's 1970s afro. Not to pick on Kyle, because a lot of guys had outrageous hair in the '70s, but does anyone remember his hair from that era? Linc, from *The Mod Squad*, had nothing on KP It's no wonder he started tying his hair into his signature ponytail.

7. Fireball Roberts's crew cut. This was the style of his era and very practical. But it made Fireball look tough as a drill sergeant.

6. Todd Bodine's bald head. Some guys will do anything to keep their heads cool.

5. Fonty Flock's pompadour. There were a lot of guys, on and off the track, wearing this style back in the 1950s. But Flock pulled it off while also wearing a half-helmet and goggles.

4. Danica Patrick's long hair. Nobody ever looked better taking off a helmet.

3. Jeff Gordon's mullet. True, mullets were ubiquitous in the early 1980s. But these days, it's hard to imagine Jeff sporting a hairdo described as "business in the front, party in the back."

2. Dale Earnhardt Sr.'s mustache. It was intimidating, legendary, and it made him instantly recognizable. If it wasn't trademarked, it should have been.

1. Boris Said's hair. Said's French poodle hairdo inspired a network of fans (known as Said Heads) to wear wigs in his honor as they cheered on their favorite road-course driver.

Some of NASCAR's original grand old tracks no longer host NASCAR Sprint Cup Series races. Some are gone, but none of them are forgotten. Here are a few of the tracks that helped jump-start stock car racing. Just close your eyes, feel the dust, and imagine them in black and white.

8. Oakland Stadium. The one-mile dirt oval track built in 1931 featured IndyCar races until 1936. After that, the venue known as the "fastest dirt track in the nation" hosted all kinds of races, including stock car events. In 1954, Dick Rathmann's win during a 250-lap race was the first last-place-to-first-place victory in NASCAR history.

7. Lakewood Speedway. From 1915 to 1979, the one-mile dirt track (that came complete with a lake for racing boats in the infield) in Lakewood (South Atlanta), Georgia, hosted all types of racing—from stock cars and Indy cars to motorcycles. Richard Petty almost won the first NASCAR Sprint Cup race of his career here in 1959. Lee Petty, originally thought to have finished second, protested. Judges agreed and the elder Petty got the win.

6. Hickory Speedway. Gwyn Staley won the first race at this historic short track in 1951. In 1953, NASCAR stars, including Tim Flock, who won the first NASCAR Sprint Cup event, and Junior Johnson, who won here seven times, began visiting the track regularly. Ned Jarrett, who returned to Hickory to promote races after he retired as a driver, considered this his home track. Although Hickory still runs races from a variety of series, NASCAR Sprint Cup events moved on after the 1971 season.

5. Occoneechee Speedway. This legendary oval dirt track opened for business in 1949 and closed in 1968. Of the 32 NASCAR races run at the track, Lee Petty won the most (three). The Historic Speedway Group recently renovated some of the original buildings to keep part of its history intact, though the track itself has been converted into a walking trail.

4. North Carolina Speedway. Also known as "Rockingham" or "the Rock," the old North Carolina Speedway was dropped from the NASCAR schedule (but saved from demolition) in 2007. Although the Rock won't be hosting NASCAR Sprint Cup races, NASCAR history buffs and longtime fans were happy to see the track reopen in 2009.

3. North Wilkesboro Speedway. Known as Junior Johnson's home track, this historic 5/8-mile venue hosted its first race (Bob Flock won) in 1949. During the next 48 years, 93 NASCAR premier series races were run on the rough-and-tumble track with corn growing in the infield before it was shuttered after Jeff Gordon won the final race in 1996. The track reopened in 2010, but has since been closed again.

2. Charlotte Speedway. This three-quarter mile dirt track located on Little Rock Island hosted the first-ever strictly stock car race on June 19, 1949. Bill France Sr. presented winner Jim Roper with the promised $5,000 purse, but only after flagged winner Glenn Dunnaway was disqualified for illegal rear springs. Today, the former track, which closed its doors in 1956, is a field between two highways near the Charlotte airport.

1. Daytona Beach & Road Course. The "track" that started it all was actually a road course that was part road (Route A1A) and part beach. The original route allowed for 3.2-mile laps, and then in the late 1940s, a 4.1-mile route (that included a two-mile straightaway) was configured. The course, a rugged run with sandy turns and deep ruts, was NASCAR's signature race site until Daytona International Speedway made its debut in 1959.

This may be considered cheating (or, as we say in racing, "innovative engineering"). But when coming up with a list of NASCAR icons, why not borrow from the NASCAR Hall of Fame? Here are the first 15 NASCAR Hall of Fame Inductees, each one a motorsports icon.

15. Cale Yarborough. Drove to three consecutive NASCAR Sprint Cup Series titles (1976-1978).

14. Glen Wood. Driver turned owner of the legendary Wood Brothers team.

13. Darrell Waltrip. Winner of 84 races and three NASCAR Sprint Cup championships.

12. Dale Inman. Set the mark for most wins and championships by a crew chief.

11. Richie Evans. Nine-time NASCAR Modified Tour champion.

10. Lee Petty. Set the bar for every driver who came after him.

9. David Pearson. The definition of a great, great driver.

8. Bud Moore. A winning owner right out of the gates, Moore's teams collected a total of 63 wins.

7. Ned Jarrett. No driver accomplished more in such a short career.

6. Bobby Allison. Scrappy, fearless, outrageous, and unforgettable.

5. Richard Petty. The undisputed King. He is an instantly recognizable ambassador for NASCAR.

4. Junior Johnson. From outlaw, to superstar driver, to powerhouse team owner, Johnson definitely left his mark.

3. Bill France Jr. His father, Big Bill, started it all. And Bill Jr. ushered NASCAR into the new millennium, making it the sports behemoth that it is.

2. Bill France Sr. Drivers used to joke that Big Bill held his board meetings in a phone booth. No question, it was his way or the highway. But he was the pioneer and driving force behind the sport.

1. Dale Earnhardt Sr. More than just NASCAR's Intimidator, Earnhardt was—and still is—beloved worldwide.

Call it sports lore. Every sport has old stories and legends that are told over and over again, and then get passed down to members of the next generation, who, in turn, keep telling the stories. Sometimes, these legends are embellished. Who knows if they are completely true? And who cares? These are our stories, and we're sticking to them.

17. Deal unsealed. As the story goes, many years before UPS sponsored Dale Jarrett's car, the company was negotiating with another NASCAR Sprint Cup Series team. The deal was ready to be signed and sealed, but then a secretary sent the papers to execs at UPS via FedEx. End of story.

16. Rain or shine. Pocono Raceway legend has it that when it's raining in Turn 1, it's sunny in Turn 3.

15. Rude awakening. Tim Flock, the youngest of the Flock brothers racing clan, lay down to take a nap on the infield before a 1953 race in South Carolina. He missed the race—and most of the season—after a car accidentally backed over him while he was sleeping.

14. The Talladega curse. For many years, no Coors Light Pole Award winner went on to win the race at Talladega. If that was a real curse, it's since been broken many times by pole sitter/winners Bill Elliott (1987), Dale Earnhardt Sr. (1990), Sterling Marlin (1995), Bobby Labonte (1998), and Jeff Gordon (2007). It used to also be said that no driver who scored his first-ever NASCAR Sprint Cup win at Talladega would win again at any track. But Davey Allison (followed by Ken Schrader, Brian Vickers, and Brad Keselowski) squelched that myth.

13. Hot dog. Everyone loves Martinsville hot dogs, but Dale Earnhardt Sr. allegedly used to eat several chili dogs right before making his qualifying run to give himself "extra octane."

12. Bunk buddies. When they were just starting out and traveling from track to track, Tiny Lund and Cale Yarborough frequently slept on a mattress in the back of Lund's Pontiac station wagon.

11. Lighting up the track. Heavy smoker Dick Trickle drilled a hole in his race helmet so he could smoke during races. He also installed cigarette lighters in his car (which were not standard in race cars). People vouch for this story.

10. Got goats? When his dad, Ned, got him a job as groundskeeper at Hickory Motor Speedway in the early 1970s, Dale Jarrett brought in a herd of goats to take care of the lawn.

9. The legendary John Lentz. When Ned Jarrett first started racing short tracks, his father, Homer, didn't approve. So Ned raced under the name of his racing partner, John Lentz. When "Lentz" kept winning races and became the talk of the short-track circuit, Ned's father confronted him.

To Ned's surprise, his father, a sawmill worker, told him that if he was going to win, he should continue to race and start using his real name. And he did.

8. Good on paper. Long before Dale Earnhardt Jr. was a driver, Rick Hendrick asked him if he had a contract with anyone. Junior said no. Hendrick wrote out a contract on a napkin and Junior signed it.

7. Off course. Before he was a full-time driver, Cale Yarborough took a part-time gig as a skydiver for South Carolina's Beaufort Water Festival. The plan was for him to jump from 10,000 feet and land in Port Royal Sound, where a boat would pick him up. Instead, Yarborough drifted into town and landed on top of a dentist's office.

6. Thumbing it. While competing in the first-ever stock-car race in Charlotte in 1949, Lee Petty flipped his car. The crumpled car was one of two vehicles that Petty and a group of family and friends had driven from Level Cross, North Carolina, to the track. The women in the group drove home in the working car. Lee stayed to get the other car fixed, while his son, Richard, hitchhiked all the way home.

5. Star-studded. At the first race at Darlington Raceway in 1950, over 25,000 fans showed up the night before the race. Because there was only one hotel in town back then, most of them slept in their cars or outside in the town square, under the stars.

4. Impromptu landing. Once, while piloting his own plane, Curtis Turner, who was running late for the race at Darlington, purposely passed the local airport and landed on the track's backstretch.

3. Seeing red. In the early days of NASCAR, drivers would pack cold drinks in their cars to help hydrate during the long, hot races. At one particular race at Darlington, Buck Baker brought a gallon jug of cold tomato juice. When he wrecked, the tomato juice was splattered everywhere, giving emergency workers an initial scare when they helped him—unhurt for the most part—from his car.

2. Pickled. Dale Earnhardt Jr. hydrates with pickle juice before exceptionally hot races. It also helps hangovers, or so Junior told reporters.

1. Very tacky. Legend has it that Curtis Turner once flew over a track where his rival Speedy Thompson was competing and dropped a carton of tacks onto the racing surface.

The Mark Martin Award (and More Notable Runner-Up Stats)

Mark Martin is, without a doubt, one of the greatest and most respected drivers in NASCAR history. However, he had a knack for finishing second—in races and in points. As Dale Earnhardt used to say, "You finish second, then you're just the first loser." True. But you still beat 41 guys. With the level of competition these days, that's not too shabby.

Here are some of NASCAR's great all-time bridesmaids (including Mark Martin)—drivers who have finished second in the NASCAR Sprint Cup Series championship points race the most times. All but Martin and James Hylton have gone on to win one or more championships.

9. James Hylton. Three-time runner-up (zero championships).

8. Bill Elliott. Three-time runner-up (one-time champion).

7. Herb Thomas. Three-time runner-up (two-time champion).

6. Cale Yarborough. Three-time runner-up (three-time champion).

5. Darrell Waltrip. Three-time runner-up (three-time champion).

4. Dale Earnhardt Sr. Three-time runner-up (seven-time champion).

3. Mark Martin. Five-time runner-up (zero championships).

2. Bobby Allison. Five-time runner-up (one-time champion).

1. Richard Petty. Six-time runner-up (seven-time champion).

Bonus: More Notable NASCAR Runner-Up Stats

4. Rusty Wallace. In his first-ever NASCAR race in Atlanta in 1980, Wallace crossed the finish line second, just nine seconds behind the winner, Dale Earnhardt Sr.

3. Clint Bowyer. When Bowyer finished behind Jimmie Johnson by 0.002 seconds at Talladega in 2011, he tied Kurt Busch (who finished behind Ricky Craven by the same margin at Darlington in 2003) for the closest second-place finish in a NASCAR Sprint Cup points race since the advent of electronic scoring.

2. James Hylton. He placed second more times (12) than any NASCAR Sprint Cup driver before he finally won a NASCAR Sprint Cup race in 1970. Harry Gant is just behind him with 10 second-place finishes.

1. Dale Earnhardt Sr. He finished second in the Daytona 500 four times (in 1984, 1993, 1995, and 1996) before he finally won it in 1998. He finished second again the following year, making him a five-time Daytona 500 bridesmaid.

Race fans are passionate about many things, including the procurement of NASCAR merchandise. Kyle Petty once said, "If we made NASCAR doggie floss, fans would buy it." NASCAR does lend its officially licensed logo to a variety of products from lip balm to fresh fruit bouquets.

More often than not, fans collect swag to show their devotion to their favorite driver. NASCAR enthusiasts have dedicated entire rooms to Darrell Waltrip, Tony Stewart, or the Earnhardts. A Jeff Gordon fan named Charlotte Simpson collected 2,000 Gordon die-cast cars and donated them to the NASCAR Hall of Fame. Winners of the Official NASCAR Members Club Biggest Fan contest, Russ and Julie Geary, painted their aboveground pool to resemble paint schemes of top drivers. There are many, many stories like this.

It's hard to imagine now, but in the early days of the sport many great drivers, including the King, tried unsuccessfully to market their image. The man who finally got it right was Dale Earnhardt Sr., who basically wrote the book on NASCAR merchandising.

With all the other cool stuff out there (some favorites are listed below), who knows who next year's top seller will be?

25. Clint Bowyer travel tumbler.

24. Jeff Gordon lunch box. Or, even better, sling six-can cooler.

23. NASCAR Hall of Fame Yearbook.

22. Greg Biffle large pet bandana. For big dogs only.

21. One-inch adjustable Jeff Gordon dog collar.

20. Denny Hamlin FedEx replica uniform jacket.

19. Ryan Newman soft-sided coolers.

18. Tony Stewart truck mud flaps.

17. Mark Martin connecting rod key chain.

16. Jimmie Johnson No. 48 leash, collar, and ID tag set. For your pup.

15. Carl Edwards deluxe grill cover.

14. Kyle Busch comfy throw with sleeves. Since it's a blanket with sleeves, fans can cuddle up and still keep their hands free to use the TV remote and grab some M&Ms.

13. No. 88 pajamas. In Dale Jr. green.

12. Chase for the NASCAR Sprint Cup Beverage Coozies.

11. NASCAR scanners. Allows fans to listen to in-race driver audio.

10. Intimidator clock. Check out the mustache.

9. Danica Patrick laptop skin.

8. Kevin Harvick temporary tattoo. For fans not quite ready to commit.

7. Jeff Gordon trifold wallet. Sorry, not his actual wallet.

6. Matt Kenseth plush car.

5. Joey Logano 10K yellow gold flip flop pendant.

4. Tony Stewart Smoke barbeque sauce.

3. Framed piece of used tire from Tony Stewart's Brickyard win in 2005.

2. Junior Johnson's Midnight Moon beverage. It's 80-proof, made legally, and very tasty over ice.

1. Piece of Daytona International Speedway asphalt. When the track was repaved in 2010, fans snapped up chunks of asphalt from the track, which hadn't been paved since 1978, in one of more than 20 collectible versions.

NASCAR on TV is one thing. NASCAR on the big screen is quite another. Here are our picks for the all-time best, worst and ugliest racing movies.

The Good

7. *The Dale Earnhardt Story.* Actor Barry Pepper did a good job playing the Intimidator, a tough bill to fill. Not bad for a TV movie actor tackling a major icon of NASCAR.

6. *Cannonball Run.* It's another Burt Reynolds vehicle in the *Stroker Ace/Smokey and the Bandit* realm. Some consider this movie a racing classic, even though there's no race track and the "car" driven by the stars in the cross-country race is an ambulance. However, there is a street-legal version of Donnie Allison's Hawaiian Tropic race car driven by Terry Bradshaw and Mel Tillis.

5. *The Ride of Their Lives.* This NASCAR documentary, narrated by Kevin Costner, is a must-see DVD with great interviews and historical footage.

4. *Talladega Nights: The Ballad of Ricky Bobby.* Pure Will Ferrell silliness.

3. *NASCAR 3D: The IMAX Experience.* The next best thing to being there.

2. *Cars.* As a NASCAR fan, you've got to like a movie in which a race car named Lightning McQueen (voice by Owen Wilson) is the star. Voiceovers by Richard Petty (as the King), Darrell Waltrip (as Darrell Cartrip), and other drivers, including Dale Earnhardt Jr., make it a classic.

1. *Days of Thunder.* This big-budget movie put NASCAR on the pop culture map in a big way. It began as the idea of hard-core racing fan Tom Cruise, who starred as driver Cole Trickle. The team owner and crew chief characters played by Randy Quaid and Robert Duvall were based on Cruise's buddies, Rick Hendrick and Harry Hyde.

The Bad

4. *Thunder in Carolina.* A B movie with a story line based around the old Southern 500 race in Darlington, South Carolina. At least the vintage 1959 racing footage is pretty cool.

3. *Stroker Ace.* Although this movie, which features a driver played by Burt Reynolds battling with his fried chicken mogul sponsor, gets extra points for showcasing Loni Anderson (as a straitlaced schoolteacher) and actress Cassandra Peterson (who later became known as Elvira), we still have to give it a thumbs down. All the cameos by drivers, including Kyle Petty, Dale Earnhardt Sr., Neil Bonnett, and Harry Gant, as well as one by broadcaster Ken Squier, almost reversed the decision, but looking back, it's pretty bad.

2. *Days of Thunder.* This flick also makes the "bad" list because, although it was a box office hit with big stars, critics trashed it as a *Top Gun* rehash and many NASCAR insiders cringed at some of its inconsistencies. You either love it or hate it. Or you love to hate it.

1. *Speedway.* Like a car wreck. Bad, but you just can't look away. (Note to Elvis: there's only one King in NASCAR.)

Best Cameos

2. The King. In the 2008 Kevin Costner movie, *Swing Vote*, Costner's character, Bud, whose vote will decide the presidential election, gets a ride from Richard Petty in his famous No. 43.

1. The Intimidator. In the Trey Parker movie, *BASEketball*, Earnhardt played himself driving a cab with the famous No. 3 on its side.

Everybody says "The Star-Spangled Banner" is one of the most challenging songs to sing, so you've got to hand it to anyone brave enough to try it in front of thousands of fans at a race track while millions of other people are also watching on TV.

From unknowns, to rising stars, to military quartets, many have performed the national anthem at NASCAR events, and some have delivered great renditions. Here are some of the best of them from over the years.

10. Engelbert Humperdinck, singer (Daytona International Speedway, 1996 Daytona 500). The guy can sing.

9. Mariah Carey, singer (Daytona International Speedway, 2003 Daytona 500). Gotta love those high notes.

8. John Schneider, original *Dukes of Hazzard* actor (Memphis Motorsports Park, 2006). Who knew Bo Duke could sing?

7. Fergie, singer (Daytona International Speedway, 2006 Daytona 500). When it's the Black Eyed Peas' Fergie, and not the Duchess of York Fergie, you've got no complaints.

6. Billy Ray Cyrus, singer/actor (Bristol Motor Speedway, 2011). Forget his mullet-wearing past. Hannah Montana's dad can definitely carry his own tune.

5. Darius Rucker, singer (Charlotte Motor Speedway, 2010). As the enormous new Jumbotron broadcast a flapping American flag and a Stealth Bomber flew overhead, the ex-Hootie and the Blowfish front man delivered a smoker.

4. Vanessa Williams, actress/singer (Daytona International Speedway, 2005 Daytona 500). Serious pipes.

3. Trisha Yearwood, singer (Daytona International Speedway, 2008 Daytona 500). More serious pipes.

2. Harry Connick Jr., singer/actor (Daytona International Speedway, 2010 Daytona 500). A personal favorite.

1. Jim Cornelison, full-time national anthem singer for the Chicago Blackhawks (Chicagoland Speedway, 2010). As an ex-opera singer and the guy who performs "The Star-Spangled Banner" (as well as "O Canada") regularly, he has an edge. But he's really good.

One-Hit Wonders

In the "Way-Back Machine," it used to be tremendously difficult to win a NASCAR Sprint Cup Series race because you had to beat Richard Petty to do it. These days, NASCAR's premier series is full of winners (182 and counting), and in this group, nearly one-third (62) of the drivers have just one NASCAR Sprint Cup win to their credit.

We call these drivers "One-Hit Wonders." But it's important to note that every one of these single-timers did something most people can only dream about: win at NASCAR's top level. So, let's give these drivers their due, in alphabetical order.

62. Johnny Allen

61. Marcos Ambrose

60. Bill Amick

59. Mario Andretti

58. Earl Balmer

57. Trevor Bayne

56. Johnny Benson

55. Brett Bodine

54. Ron Bouchard

53. Richard Brickhouse

52. Dick Brooks

51. Bob Burdick

50. Marvin Burke

49. Neil Cole

48. Jim Cook

47. Mark Donohue

46. Joe Eubanks

45. Lou Figaro

44. Jimmy Florian

43. Larry Frank

42. Danny Graves

41. Royce Haggerty

40. Bobby Hillin Jr.

39. Jim Hurtubise

38. John Kieper

37. Harold Kite

36. Paul Lewis

35. Joey Logano

34. Johnny Mantz

33. Sam McQuagg

32. Casey Mears

31. Paul Menard

30. Lloyd Moore

29. Jerry Nadeau

28. Norm Nelson

27. Bill Norton

26. Phil Parsons

25. Dick Passwater

24. Lennie Pond

23. David Ragan

22. Bill Rexford

21. Jody Ridley

20. Shorty Rollins

19. Jim Roper

18. Earl Ross

17. John Rostek

16. Johnny Rutherford

15. Greg Sacks

14. Leon Sales

13. Frankie Schneider

12. Wendell Scott

11. Buddy Shuman

10. Regan Smith

9. John Soares

8. Lake Speed

7. Chuck Stevenson

6. Donald Thomas

5. Tommy Thompson

4. Martin Truex Jr.

3. Art Watts

2. Danny Weinberg

1. Jack White

Some wins by one-hit wonders are more memorable than others.

9. Richard Brickhouse (Talladega Superspeedway, Talladega, Alabama, September 14, 1969). While many of NASCAR's top drivers boycotted the first-ever race at Talladega due to concerns about the over-the-top speed of the new track, Brickhouse chose to race that day and took the checkered flag. Unfortunately for Brickhouse, some of the sport's top drivers held his decision to race against him and he only ran in a dozen or so more races before retiring.

8. Lake Speed (Darlington Raceway, Darlington, South Carolina, March 27, 1988). When your last name is Speed, you have to make the list. Speed's sole win was part of a career where he notched 75 top 10 finishes.

7. Ron Bouchard (Talladega Superspeedway, Talladega, Alabama, August 2, 1981). Bouchard hit the NASCAR Sprint Cup Series in 1981 and took Rookie of the Year honors at season's end. At the time, his win at Talladega—in a thrilling three-wide finish alongside Darrell Waltrip and Terry Labonte—made him only the third rookie to win a NASCAR Sprint Cup race since 1957.

6. Buddy Shuman (Stamford Park, Niagara Falls, Ontario, July 1, 1952). Shuman, a true NASCAR pioneer, took his first and only win at NASCAR's first Canadian-based race, finishing a full two laps ahead of the pack.

5. Shorty Rollins (State Line Speedway, Busti, New York, July 16, 1958). Rookie of the Year in 1958, Rollins beat out some heavy hitters, including Lee Petty, to take his first and only NASCAR Sprint Cup race during his first year of competition. Shorty also has the distinction of winning the first-ever race at Daytona, where he took the checkered flag at the qualifying race for the inaugural Daytona 500 in 1959.

4. Trevor Bayne (Daytona International Speedway, Daytona Beach, Florida, February 20, 2011). Bayne garnered his win at the most prestigious race of the year in only his second-ever NASCAR Sprint Cup start.

3. Phil Parsons (Talladega Superspeedway, Talladega, Alabama, May 1, 1988).
During his debut season of 1983, Parsons failed to finish the race in Talladega, following an 11-car pileup. In 1988, the best season of his career in which he ultimately finished ninth in points, Parsons got his sole NASCAR Sprint Cup win at the track he claimed as his favorite despite the rumored Talladega curse following first-time winners.

2. Jim Hurtubise (Atlanta Motor Speedway, Atlanta, Georgia, March 27, 1966).
Hurtubise took on cult-hero status when, following a 1964 IndyCar crash, he insisted that his doctors surgically sculpt his hands so he could grip the wheel of a car. A few years later, he won his first and only NASCAR race a full two miles ahead of champion Fred Lorenzen.

1. Wendell Scott (Jacksonville Speedway Park, Jacksonville, Florida, December 1, 1963).
Scott's single NASCAR Sprint Cup win, the first by an African-American, would have been remarkable on its own. But his win came in a NASCAR Sprint Cup run that lasted 12 years, with Scott logging 147 top 10 finishes, despite struggling against underfunding and poor equipment.

It's hard these days to get most people to donate to charities for humans. It's even harder when the charitable causes have to do with helping animals. But the NASCAR community gives back like no other. The Greg Biffle Foundation (gregbifflefoundation.com) and Ryan Newman Foundation (ryannewmanfoundation.org) both help animals in a huge way. NASCAR people love their pets, and here are a few of the drivers who give a whole new meaning to dogleg turn.

13. Greg Biffle. Driver and big-time dog lover, the Biff, is often seen out and about with his boxers, Foster, Gracie, and Savannah.

12. Jeff Burton. At last count, Burton's family had 49 pets, including rabbits, guinea pigs, hamsters, horses, frogs, cats, a dog, and lots of fish.

11. Kurt Busch. Although he has three great dogs (Ginger, Lola, and Jim), Busch says his horses (Lauro and CJ) give him a sense of calm. As long as he steers clear of the odors of the barn.

10. Dale Earnhardt Jr. Besides his two dogs—a boxer named Killer (the son of Greg Biffle's dog, Foster) and a Great Dane named Stroker Ace (named for the Burt Reynolds movie character)—and his two cats (Buddy and Tux), Junior keeps a pair of buffalo (Laverne and Shirley) and three Texas longhorns (Lindy Lou, Dance 'till Dawn and Shadows Tiger Lily).

9. Tim Flock. In the early 1950s, Tim Flock brought his pet rhesus monkey, Jocko Flocko, to the track and even let him ride along in his race car a few times. Then, in the middle of a race, the monkey caused a ruckus and forced Flock to pit and forfeit the lead. After that, Jocko Flocko was a stay-at-home monkey.

8. Jeff Green. His two Labradors are aptly named Short Track and Vegas.

7. Rick Hendrick. Watch what you say around George, this team owner's parrot.

6. Jimmie Johnson. A shih-tzu named Roxanne and a havanese named Maya are the five-time champ's canines of choice.

5. Casey Mears. At home, Mears's chase is between his cats, Gus and Rags, and his miniature Australian shepherd, Kya.

4. Ryan Newman. The Newman family's six-dog menagerie includes Mopar, Harley, Fred, Digger, Dunkin, and Socks.

3. Elliott Sadler. To prepare for hunting season, Sadler trains his 50 Tennessee walker coonhounds in a fox preserve.

2. Tony Stewart. The second driver to own a monkey (Stewart's is named Mojo), Stewart also has a rotating pet roster that includes a parrot, two cats (Wylie and Wyatt), a Chihuahua named Kayle, and a tiger, which is kept in a Charlotte, North Carolina, zoo.

1. Joe Weatherly. In the late 1950s and early 1960s, Weatherly used to bring a mongoose to the track because he was deathly afraid of snakes. That counts as a pet, right?

Kings of the Road

There are currently two road courses on the NASCAR Sprint Cup Series circuit, Watkins Glen International and Infineon Raceway. Some of us love road-course racing; it's an occasional right turn for the left-turn league. It's also a change of scenery and a true test of man and machine.

Road-course races are an opportunity to see the road-course specialists at work. Boris Said is a champion in his own right; the same goes for Ron Fellows, Scott Pruett, and Dan Gurney. Great drivers, and great guys, by the way.

Road-course races used to be throwaways, but now, if you want to be a NASCAR Sprint Cup champion, you have to be a great road-course driver.

Jeff Gordon and Tony Stewart are the undisputed kings of the road course. But there are always the hired guns who give the regulars a run for their money on every road course. Here are the drivers with the most all-time road-course wins.

6. Three-time winners. Geoffrey Bodine, Tim Flock, Ernie Irvan, Cale Yarborough.

5. Four-time winners. Mark Martin, David Pearson.

4. Five-time winners. Dan Gurney, Tim Richmond, Darrell Waltrip.

3. Six-time winners. Bobby Allison, Richard Petty, Ricky Rudd, Rusty Wallace.

2. Seven-time winner. Tony Stewart.

1. Nine-time winner. Jeff Gordon.

At the beginning of NASCAR's modern era in the early 1970s, single-car teams were the norm. By the mid-1990s, powerhouse multicar teams such as Hendrick Motorsports and Roush Fenway Racing began to rule the day. Even though a few small outfits, such as Morgan-McClure Motorsports, scored big wins during the last 17 years (Sterling Marlin won the Daytona 500 in 1994 and 1995), teams running with just one car found themselves at a competitive disadvantage, and became fewer and farther between (note the over six-year gap between the 2003 and 2009 wins in the list below).

Flying solo is an incredible challenge in racing. Here are the seven NASCAR Sprint Cup Series wins, so far, by single-car teams since 2001.

7. May 7, 2011. Regan Smith, Furniture Row Racing, Darlington Raceway.

6. February 20, 2011. Trevor Bayne, Wood Brothers Racing, Daytona International Speedway.

5. April 26, 2009. Brad Keselowski, Phoenix Racing, Talladega Superspeedway.

4. March 16, 2003. Ricky Craven, PPI Motorsports, Darlington Raceway.

2. February 17, 2002. Ward Burton, Bill Davis Racing, Daytona International Speedway.

2. October 15, 2001. Ricky Craven, PPI Motorsports, Martinsville Speedway.

1. March 25, 2001. Elliott Sadler, Wood Brothers Racing, Bristol Motor Speedway.

Standout Truck Races

The NASCAR Camping World Truck Series ran its inaugural race at Phoenix International Raceway in 1995. Today, more than a half million people tune in for each televised race. Fans get to watch a field of competitors made up of truck specialists, such as Todd Bodine, Ron Hornaday Jr., and Johnny Sauter, as well as NASCAR Nationwide and NASCAR Sprint Cup Series regulars, many of whom—including Carl Edwards and Greg Biffle—got their big breaks racing trucks. Here are some NASCAR Camping World Truck Series races we won't soon forget.

6. Texas Motor Speedway (2010). Despite the distraction of several late cautions, Todd Bodine held off Ron Hornaday Jr., Johnny Sauter, and Austin Dillon in the final laps to grab the win.

5. Talladega Superspeedway (2010). The three-wide finish, with Kyle Busch edging out Aric Almirola (followed closely by Johnny Sauter) by 0.002 seconds not only marked the second closest finish in NASCAR Camping World Truck Series history, but it was also the second consecutive year in which Busch and Almirola marked a one-two finish.

4. Kansas Speedway (2011). The 2011 Kansas race, number 400 for the series, showcased plenty of action. At one point, side-by-side competitors Johnny Sauter and Ron Hornaday Jr. both turned their trucks sideways at 60-degree angles at the same time without wrecking each other.

3. Nashville Superspeedway (2009). When four-time NASCAR Camping World Truck champ Ron Hornaday Jr. won the race at Nashville, he became the first NASCAR driver in 38 years to win five consecutive races (at Milwaukee, Memphis, Kentucky, O'Reilly Raceway Park at Indianapolis, and Nashville). He also joined Bobby Allison in a tie for third on the consecutive wins list.

2. Daytona International Speedway (2000). Mike Wallace steered clear of a spectacular crash—involving Geoffrey Bodine and 11 others—and won the first truck race run at Daytona.

1. Colorado National Raceway (1995). Butch Miller beat Mike Skinner by 0.001 seconds in what remains the closest finish in NASCAR Camping World Truck Series history.

When it comes to stumping for their sponsors, nobody does it better than NASCAR drivers. There are dozens of good TV commercials featuring NASCAR drivers. Here are a dozen on-air ads we definitely won't forget.

12. Tony Stewart for Burger King. Smoke worked all kinds of jobs before he became a NASCAR Sprint Cup Series champion, but actually seeing him flip burgers and work the drive-thru window at Burger King makes for a great ad. A close second was the spot where he takes a lie detector test to prove that he really loves the Whopper.

11. Richard Petty for Goody's. Any commercial where the King says "Goody's" is a favorite.

10. Dick Trickle for NAPA Auto Parts. In this 1997 spot, Trickle good-naturedly poked fun at his lack of success in NASCAR Sprint Cup competition when he announced a contest with a $100,000 prize for the fan who picked the winner of that season's NAPA 500 race.

"A little tip," said Trickle. "It's gonna be me." An on-screen graphic ("Dick is 0 for 243 in Cup races") counseled otherwise.

9. Jeff Gordon for Nextel. The combination of Gordon driving a throwback Chevy convertible, rocking out to Deep Purple, and running out of gas as cars, trucks, and an old man on a bike pass him by is a winning combination.

8. Tony Stewart, Denny Hamlin, Kyle Busch, and Michael Waltrip for Toyota. Kids use a remote to control the drivers' on-track moves. Mayhem ensues.

7. Michael Waltrip and Dale Earnhardt Jr. for Domino's. The pizza guy shows up at the garage and announces a delivery for "Mr. NASCAR." Both Jr. and Mikey say, "That's me." They keep one-upping each other until Junior gets the last words, "King Daddy!"

6. Joey Logano for The Home Depot. When Logano hit the home improvement store to stock up on everything he needs to win a championship (a car, a crew, fans), The Home Depot had a hit.

5. Jimmie Johnson for Kobalt. Along with his crew chief, Chad Knaus, Jimmie Johnson escapes being crushed by a car falling off a lift when a sturdy Kobalt toolbox breaks the fall.

4. Greg Biffle for Double Stuf Oreos. The Biff's "ready, set, lick" contest with a woman we assume is his grandmother is hilarious.

3. Michael Waltrip for NAPA Auto Parts. It starts wistful and ends silly when Mikey realizes, "I'm at the wrong track."

2. Dale Jarrett for UPS. Costars Martin Truex Jr., Kyle Petty, and Bobby Labonte accompany Jarrett on his last spin in the UPS truck. Brings a tear to your eye when the screen reads, "Thanks Dale. It's been a great ride."

1. Richard Petty and Kyle Petty for the NASCAR Ride -Along Program on ESPN. The King's backseat driving is priceless.

In no other sport are players—in this case, drivers—so closely identified with their sponsors.

When you think of the King, you think of STP Oil Treatment. When you think of Jeff Gordon, the colors of the DuPont rainbow spring to mind.

In the 1950s and 1960s, NASCAR sponsors were mostly companies that made cars or automotive products. Then in the 1970s, consumer products, such as Tide and Coca-Cola, jumped on board. More recently, financial, medical, communications, and technology firms have come along for the ride. These days, it's not unusual to see a car promoting a movie release or a campaign, such as Thank a Teacher Today or Drive to End Hunger.

From the Heluva Good! Sour Cream Dips 400 to the Pork the Other White Meat 400, race events and race teams welcome any and all sponsors. But over the years there have been some unusual driver-product pairings. Here are some we never expected.

12. Powerpuff Girls. The girls were featured on a car sponsored by the Cartoon Network. Who knows? Maybe it inspired a nation of future Danicas.

11. The Muppets. The fans liked it, and it pays to start 'em young.

10. M&Ms Pretzel. Three words you never thought you'd hear in one sentence: M&Ms Pretzel Toyota. But those things are tasty. M&Ms is sure getting its money's worth from Kyle Busch.

9. Little Debbie. Aussie Marcos Ambrose hands out these cute little cakes to reporters and ups the man factor by joking that one of their ingredients is koala hair.

8. Huggies. The No. 1 question people ask NASCAR drivers is how they go to the bathroom while driving in those long, long races. Just saying.

7. Kim Kardashian fragrance. The Mike Bliss-driven Chevrolet sponsored by the reality TV star's new perfume was hot pink. No report on how it smelled.

6. Viagra. Sponsorship from the company producing the popular little blue pill took some getting used to, but driver Mark Martin was an incredibly good sport about it.

5. ExtenZe. Still not quite used to it. But if two-time Super Bowl-winning coach Jimmy Johnson is comfortable talking about it, surely we'll get there soon.

4. Hooker. It's not what you think. In 1966, Buddy Baker's car was sponsored by John Jay Hooker, who was running for governor in Tennessee. Baker's No. 00 was overlapped with the "oo" letters in Hooker's name, which ran down the side of the car.

3. Midnight Moon Carolina Moonshine. Sold in liquor stores, Junior Johnson's product is completely legal. But it's still ironic to see a moonshine logo splashed across the hood of a stock car.

2. Racing for Jesus. Does Morgan Shepherd's NASCAR Nationwide Series car have an unfair advantage?

1. Boudreaux's Butt Paste. We did not make this up.

Young Guns by Wendy Venturini

Wendy Venturini serves as a reporter for *NASCAR RaceDay* on SPEED. The daughter of two-time ARCA champion Bill Venturini and sister of ARCA driver Billy Venturini, Wendy graduated in 2000 from the University of North Carolina. Soon after, she went to work as a TV reporter in Mooresville, North Carolina, and soon was hosting her own racing show. She went on to produce NASCAR-related programming on TNN and FOX Sports Net before landing a producer role on SPEED's *NASCAR Victory Lane*. She later worked as a pit reporter for DirecTV's *NASCAR Hot Pass* and in 2007 became the first female to call a NASCAR race from the TV booth.

As a new mom, Wendy is well-qualified to talk about babies. So here is Wendy's list, from "oldest" to youngest, of the eight youngest race winners in NASCAR Sprint Cup Series history.

8. Jeff Gordon (22 years, 298 days). Charlotte Motor Speedway, May 29, 1994.

7. Richard Petty (22 years, 241 days). Southern State Fairgrounds (Charlotte, North Carolina), February 28, 1960.

6. Bobby Hillin Jr. (22 years, 52 days). Talladega Superspeedway, July 27, 1986.

5. Fireball Roberts (21 years, 205 days). Occoneechee Speedway, August 13, 1950.

4. Donald Thomas (20 years, 129 days). Lakewood Speedway, November 16, 1952.

3. Kyle Busch (20 years, 126 days). Auto Club Speedway, September 4, 2005. (Note: Kyle Busch won a NASCAR Camping World Truck Series race when he was 20 years, 18 days.)

2. Trevor Bayne (20 years, 1 day). Daytona International Speedway, February 20, 2011.

1. Joey Logano (19 years, 34 days). New Hampshire Motor Speedway, June 28, 2009. (Note: Joey Logano won a NASCAR Nationwide Series race when he was 18 years, 21 days, which underscores his status as top young gun.)

When asked why he and his brother, Jeff, have such different accents, Ward Burton said, "He lived in the northern end of the house and I lived in the southern end."

They say racing is in your blood, and nowhere is that more evident than in NASCAR's top series. From the Allisons and the Busches, to the Labontes and the Waltrips, brother combos have raced together throughout the history of the sport.

Sometimes, brothers follow in each other's footsteps, such as 1981 and 1988 Rookies of the Year, Ron and Ken Bouchard. Other times, it's car-to-car competition. And at times, the on-track sibling rivalries get heated.

When Kyle and Kurt Busch got together at the NASCAR Sprint All-Star Race, they held a grudge, so much so that they were feuding all the way to the next Thanksgiving. It was their grandmother who finally stepped in and said, "Enough is enough." After that, they let it go.

We've also seen brothers stick together. In 1998, Kenny Wallace pushed his brother, Rusty, to victory and a brotherly one-two finish during the Budweiser Shootout at Daytona. At the Daytona 500 the following week, the Labonte brothers, Terry and Bobby, both started the race in the front row. In fact, the Labontes both won NASCAR Sprint Cup Series championships and remain the only brothers to do so.

For good, bad, or ugly, here are NASCAR's brother combos with the most total NASCAR Sprint Cup wins (as of August 27, 2011).

9. Bodine (19). Geoffrey (18), Brett (1).

8. Parsons (22). Benny (21), Phil (1).

7. Burton (26). Jeff (21), Ward (5).

6. Labonte (43). Terry (22), Bobby (21). (Note: both won NASCAR Sprint Cup Series championships.)

5. Busch (46). Kurt (23), Kyle (23).

4. Thomas (49). Herb (48), Donald (1).

3. Flock (62). Tim (39), Fonty (19), Bob (4).

2. Waltrip (88). Darrell (84), Michael (4). (Note: both won the Daytona 500.)

1. Allison (94). Bobby (84), Donnie (10).

In the history of NASCAR, four sets of brothers have teamed up to win four NASCAR Sprint Cup Series races in a row: Tim, Bob, and Fonty Flock (1952); Herb and Donald Thomas (1952); Tim and Fonty Flock (1955); and Kurt and Kyle Busch (2008). Here are the brother combinations who have won back-to-back NASCAR Sprint Cup races during their careers.

8. Brett and Geoffrey Bodine. One time (1990).

7. Bob and Fonty Flock. One time (1952).

6. Donald and Herb Thomas. One time (1952).

5. Bobby and Donnie Allison. One time (1978).

4. Tim and Bob Flock. Two times (1951, 1952).

3. Bobby and Terry Labonte. Two times (both in 1995).

2. Tim and Fonty Flock. Three times (1955 back-to-back-to-back, 1956).

1. Kurt and Kyle Busch. Four times (2005, 2008, 2009, 2010).

No book of lists would be complete without a ranking of who has won the most NASCAR Sprint Cup Series races. No doubt, fans are familiar with the drivers with the most wins. But check out the middle of the pack and all the competitors with one, two, and three wins. A few of the 182 drivers who have won at least one NASCAR Sprint Cup race just might surprise you. (Note: wins through October 2, 2011.)

44. One win. Johnny Allen, Marcos Ambrose, Bill Amick, Mario Andretti, Earl Balmer, Trevor Bayne, Johnny Benson, Brett Bodine, Ron Bouchard, Richard Brickhouse, Dick Brooks, Bob Burdick, Marvin Burke, Neil Cole, Jim Cook, Mark Donohue, Joe Eubanks, Lou Figaro, Jimmy Florian, Larry Frank, Danny Graves, Royce Haggerty, Bobby Hillin Jr., Jim Hurtubise, John Kieper, Harold Kite, Paul Lewis, Joey Logano, Johnny Mantz, Sam McQuagg, Casey Mears, Paul Menard, Lloyd Moore, Jerry Nadeau, Norm Nelson, Bill Norton, Phil Parsons, Dick Passwater, Lennie Pond, David Ragan, Bill Rexford, Jody Ridley, Shorty Rollins, Jim Roper, Earl Ross, John Rostek, Johnny Rutherford, Greg Sacks, Leon Sales, Frankie Schneider, Wendell Scott, Buddy Shuman, Regan Smith, John Soares, Lake Speed, Chuck Stevenson, Donald Thomas, Tommy Thompson, Martin Truex Jr., Art Watts, Danny Weinberg, Jack White.

43. Two wins. John Andretti, Johnny Beauchamp, Red Byron, Derrike Cope, Ricky Craven, Ray Elder, James Hylton, Bobby Johns, Joe Lee Johnson, Al Keller, Elmo Langley, Danny Letner, Juan Pablo Montoya, Billy Myers, Jimmy Pardue, Steve Park, Tom Pistone, Marvin Porter, David Reutimann, Gober Sosebee, Jimmy Spencer, Brian Vickers, Emanuel Zervakis.

42. Three wins. Bill Blair, Robby Gordon, Dick Linder, Frank Mundy, Elliott Sadler, Gwyn Staley.

41. Four wins. Clint Bowyer, Lloyd Dane, Bob Flock, Charlie Glotzbach, Eddie Gray, Bobby Hamilton, Pete Hamilton, Parnelli Jones, Brad Keselowski, Hershel McGriff, Joe Nemechek, Eddie Pagan, Ken Schrader, Morgan Shepherd, Nelson Stacy, Billy Wade, Michael Waltrip, Glen Wood.

40. Five wins. Ward Burton, Dan Gurney, Alan Kulwicki, Tiny Lund, Dave Marcis, Jeremy Mayfield, Ralph Moody.

39. Six wins. Jamie McMurray.

38. Seven wins. Darel Dieringer, A.J. Foyt, Jim Reed, Marshall Teague.

37. Eight wins. Kyle Petty.

36. Nine wins. Paul Goldsmith, Cotton Owens, Bob Welborn.

35. Ten wins. Donnie Allison, Sterling Marlin.

34. Eleven wins. Kasey Kahne.

33. Thirteen wins. Dick Rathmann, Tim Richmond.

32. Fourteen wins. Dick Hutcherson, LeeRoy Yarbrough.

31. Fifteen wins. Ernie Irvan, Ryan Newman.

30. Sixteen wins. Greg Biffle.

29. Seventeen wins. Denny Hamlin, Marvin Panch, Curtis Turner.

28. Eighteen wins. Geoffrey Bodine, Neil Bonnett, Dale Earnhardt Jr., Harry Gant, Kevin Harvick.

27. Nineteen wins. Davey Allison, Buddy Baker, Carl Edwards, Fonty Flock.

26. Twenty wins. Matt Kenseth, Speedy Thompson.

25. Twenty-one wins. Jeff Burton, Bobby Labonte, Benny Parsons, Jack Smith.

24. Twenty-two wins. Terry Labonte.

23. Twenty-three wins. Kyle Busch, Ricky Rudd.

22. Twenty-four wins. Kurt Busch.

21. Twenty-five wins. Jim Paschal, Joe Weatherly.

20. Twenty-six wins. Fred Lorenzen.

19. Twenty-eight wins. Rex White.

18. Thirty-two wins. Dale Jarrett.

17. Thirty-three wins. Fireball Roberts.

16. Thirty-seven wins. Bobby Isaac.

15. Thirty-nine wins. Tim Flock.

14. Forty wins. Mark Martin.

13. Forty-one wins. Tony Stewart.

12. Forty-four wins. Bill Elliott.

11. Forty-six wins. Buck Baker.

10. Forty-eight wins. Herb Thomas.

9. Fifty wins. Ned Jarrett, Junior Johnson.

8. Fifty-four wins. Jimmie Johnson, Lee Petty.

7. Fifty-five wins. Rusty Wallace.

6. Seventy-six wins. Dale Earnhardt Sr.

5. Eighty-three wins. Cale Yarborough.

4. Eighty-four wins. Bobby Allison, Darrell Waltrip.

3. Eighty-five wins. Jeff Gordon.

2. One hundred five wins. David Pearson.

1. Two hundred wins. Richard Petty.

NASCAR has staged hundreds of great races over the years. From the first Darlington race in 1950 (when people wondered if stock cars right off the showroom floor would actually last 500 miles) to the first Daytona 500 in 1959 to the duels of the 1960s between great drivers such as Fred Lorenzen and Curtis Turner to Trevor Bayne's upset win at Daytona in 2011, there have been so many great NASCAR races that it would be impossible to list all of them.

Fans might remember a race because of a thrilling finish or because an underdog took the checkered flag. We might remember a race because it was the first-ever run under lights or because the rain poured down and wouldn't stop. With a nod to all the races we're leaving out, here are the best of the modern era (with a little help from the NASCAR Hall of Fame).

10. Daytona International Speedway (2007). Kevin Harvick beat Mark Martin to the finish line as cars went down like dominoes behind them in the Daytona 500. Harvick won by 0.02 seconds in the closest finish in the Daytona 500 since electric scoring began in 1993. Clint Bowyer's car crossed the finish line upside down, but he was unharmed.

9. Talladega Superspeedway (2000). Seven-time champ Dale Earnhardt Sr. made a miraculous comeback to win at Talladega. He methodically chose his way through the field, moving from 18th to first in the final five laps to take the checkered flag. The last of his storied career.

8. Darlington Raceway (2003). Ricky Craven edged out Kurt Busch to win. The official difference between them was 0.002 seconds—the closest finish since electronic scoring was introduced, which was tied at Talladega in 2011 by Jimmie Johnson over Clint Bowyer.

7. Michigan International Speedway (2001). When he won this exciting rain-shortened race, Sterling Marlin gained his first victory in five seasons while also giving Dodge its first NASCAR Sprint Cup Series win in 24 years.

6. Daytona International Speedway (1979). The fight (between Cale Yarborough and Donnie and Bobby Allison), the TV coverage, and a big win by the King put this race on everyone's list.

5. Phoenix International Raceway (2007). Jeff Gordon's win tied him with Dale Earnhardt Sr.'s modern-era mark of 76 career wins.

4. Talladega Superspeedway (1985). In one of the most thrilling racing comebacks ever, Bill Elliott rallied from a five-mile deficit and won at Talladega.

3. Daytona International Speedway (1976). David Pearson and Richard Petty swapped the lead four times on the final lap of the Daytona 500, and then got into a tussle in the fourth turn. Pearson managed to straighten out and sputter across the finish line first.

2. Atlanta Motor Speedway (2001). In only his third NASCAR Sprint Cup race after taking over for Dale Earnhardt Sr. on the Richard Childress Racing team, Kevin Harvick squeaked by Jeff Gordon to take the checkered flag by 0.006 seconds.

1. Daytona International Speedway (1998). Finally, finally, Dale Earnhardt Sr. got his due at the Daytona 500 that kicked off the 50th anniversary season of NASCAR. Every member of every pit crew lined up to high-five the victorious Intimidator as he savored his long, slow postrace ride to Victory Lane. What a sight.

It started with just the top 10. Now there are 12. As of the 2007 season, a dozen teams make the Chase for the NASCAR Sprint Cup and more often than not, the list of those 12 is determined following the race just before the official start of the Chase—the race at Richmond. Many say that the track at Richmond is racing perfection, so "what a perfect place for one last race to make the Chase," as they say at that storied Virginia track.

It has come down to the wire several times, as drivers poured their hearts into one final race for a shot at the Chase. Here are some of the most memorable pre-Chase races.

5. 2009. The cliff-hanger in 2009 involved Matt Kenseth, who came into the Richmond race hoping to be counted among Chase contenders for the sixth consecutive time. But Brian Vickers raced his way into the Chase that year by finishing 7th at Richmond and Kyle Busch's 5th-place finish knocked Kenseth, who finished the race in 25th place, back to 14th in the standings.

4. 2010. The story of this cutoff race was what didn't happen—Kurt Busch didn't bump race-winner Denny Hamlin out of the way for the lead. Hamlin won and both drivers cruised to the Chase along with 10 others, who stood beside them for pre-Chase photos in Victory Lane.

3. 2006. After finishing 18th at Richmond, Tony Stewart's points total put him in 11th overall place, which meant he just missed the Chase. Kasey Kahne edged him out by finishing third in the race and claiming the 10th spot.

2. 2005. Going into the race, Jamie McMurray was 10th in the standings, just one point ahead of Ryan Newman. McMurray's Lap 362 crash handed Ryan Newman his ticket to the Chase.

1. 2004. By leading 151 laps and winning the race at Richmond in 2004, Jeremy Mayfield ended a winless streak dating back to 2000. He also jumped from 14th to ninth place in points, earning him a spot in the Chase. Ryan Newman ended up in 10th place, making the Chase by a nose. But Mayfield's win knocked out Kasey Kahne, who had gone into the race eighth in points. To date, Mayfield still holds the record for overcoming the largest points deficit to make the Chase.

NASCAR fans love to watch drivers succeed. But they like it even better when a driver rises to the top of the sport for the second time, or even for the third time. There are dozens of comeback stories in NASCAR. Here are our favorites.

8. Cotton Owens. Team owner Cotton Owens showed he still had a lot of racing in him when he came out of retirement as a driver and won the 1964 Richmond race, beating his own driver, hired gun David Pearson, by a lap.

7. Mark Martin. Many people think of Mark Martin as NASCAR's elder statesman, but he may also be its comeback kid. After retiring from full-time NASCAR Sprint Cup Series competition in 2007, Martin not only returned as a full-time driver in 2009, he won five races and finished the season second in points. Despite being at the absolute top of his game in 2010 and 2011, he finished the seasons ranked only 13th and 20th. Martin plans to race again in 2012. Another comeback?

6. Steve Park. Midway through his rookie NASCAR Sprint Cup season of 1998, Dale Earnhardt Sr. protégé Steve Park was sidelined following an accident during a practice at Atlanta Motor Speedway. Seven months later, Park was back on the track. Then in 2001, he was injured in a freak caution-flag crash during a NASCAR Nationwide Series race at Darlington Raceway and sat out the rest of the season. The determined driver was again back on the track in 2002, and has since competed in both NASCAR Sprint Cup and NASCAR Camping World Truck Series races.

5. The King. Richard Petty has experienced more than his share of comebacks. As a driver, the King persevered again and again, whether he was rallying to beat David Pearson in a race or firing it up to beat Darrell Waltrip for the championship. But his greatest challenges—and comebacks—have come on the business side, where he has lost it all and rebuilt several times.

As recently as 2010, many people feared that the storied Richard Petty Enterprises would be forced to fold its tent. But the King, who at the time owned very little stock and had very little say in the business end of the company, stepped in and found investors.

Now, according to Petty, who is back calling the shots, the investors do the investing and the racing team, renamed Richard Petty Motorsports, does the racing. Sounds like a win-win.

4. Brian Vickers. In 2003, the 20-year-old Brian Vickers became the youngest NASCAR Nationwide Series champion in NASCAR history. Soon after, he was a serious NASCAR Sprint Cup competitor and in 2009, Vickers made the Chase for the NASCAR Sprint Cup for the first time in his career.

But while visiting Washington, D.C., in May 2010, Vickers fell ill. Fans were later shocked to hear Vickers had been hospitalized with blood clots in his legs, lungs, and finger. Although Vickers was sidelined for the remainder of 2010 and some of the following season while he recuperated from heart surgery to repair a hole between his left and right atrium, he returned to NASCAR Sprint Cup racing in 2011. When he skydived onto the track at Daytona, no one doubted he was back.

3. Ricky Craven. Following a wreck at Texas Motor Speedway in 1997, Craven returned to the track after missing two races. Then he stepped away from the sport for most of 1998 and struggled to reach his previous level of racing for a few seasons. But Craven bettered his precrash form in 2002, and in 2003 entered the record books when he beat Kurt Busch by 0.002 seconds at Darlington Raceway for the smallest margin of victory in a NASCAR race since the introduction of electronic scoring, which has since been tied.

2. Geoffrey Bodine. The 1986 Daytona 500 winner saw his successful career put on hold in 2000 following a NASCAR Camping World Truck Series accident. Bodine not only came back soon after, but he's still going strong (as of this writing). In fact, after qualifying for the race at Pocono in 2010, Bodine, then 61, announced his goal to be the oldest driver to win a NASCAR Sprint Cup race.

1. Ernie Irvan. In 1994, Irvan saw his successful season cut short following an accident during a practice session prior to the Michigan race. Although some had counted him out, just four months later Irvan walked onstage to accept an award for leading the most miles of competition that year—despite having missed the last 11 races of the season. He returned to racing the following season, and then in 1996 scored two wins and 16 top 10 finishes, which put him in position to finish 10th in points for the season. Even without his amazing comeback story, Irvan, who was named one of NASCAR's 50 Greatest Drivers, would be known as one of the best.

In NASCAR's early days, each team had its own scorer. The whole bunch of them would sit together in a booth and, as the story goes, they would "score" laps by taking a bean out of one jar and placing it into another jar (five beans equaled five laps). That scoring system was later upgraded to one using electronic buttons and synchronized clocks, along with cards marked by hand. In fact, that manual system is still used as a backup to the current, highly sophisticated race monitoring system.

Today, computers and electronic scoring loops embedded in track surfaces help officials keep score. Soon enough, we'll see GPS systems in race cars, leaving little doubt which car came in first in a race. But for most of NASCAR's history, human beings have been keeping track of what goes on at the track and, inevitably, mistakes have been made. Here are some of the races that, for better or for worse, are still the subject of great debate.

9. Richard Petty wins his first race . . . almost, Atlanta Motor Speedway (1959). At the finale of a one-mile dirt-track race at Lakewood Speedway near Atlanta on June 14, 1959, Richard Petty, who had yet to win a race, was flagged the winner. But the runner-up, Richard's father, Lee Petty, protested the outcome. After officials reviewed the scoring, the senior Petty was declared the winner. As the King recalled, "Because of all the dust, Daddy thought the scorers couldn't see and had docked him a lap. It took NASCAR an hour to find the error, but turns out Daddy was right."

8. Jody Ridley, Dover International Speedway (1981). The only win of Ridley's career was cloaked in controversy. Electronic timing and scoring were still years away and mistakes plagued a race that found Ridley running five laps behind leader Cale Yarborough with just 20 laps to go. Although the outcome was contested by Bobby Allison, who officially finished 22 seconds behind Ridley, the victory stood.

7. Richard Brickhouse, Talladega Superspeedway (1969). Prior to the race at Talladega, several drivers decided to boycott the race that year because of the excessive speeds being recorded at the track and the possible dangerous conditions. Richard Brickhouse crossed the picket line and won the race that day for the only win of his career.

6. Regan Smith, Talladega Superspeedway (2008). Regan Smith was ready to celebrate his first career victory, but it was not to be. As Smith sped by leader Tony Stewart in pursuit of the checkered flag, he passed below the yellow line, which negated his win and pushed him back to an 18th-place finish. Smith claimed he was forced below the line and if NASCAR had agreed, it would have been up to the judges to decide if the win was his. As it stood, Smith had to wait three years to score his first "W"—at the Darlington race in 2011.

5. Biffle's coast (2007). At a rainy Kansas race in 2007, Greg Biffle called upon strategy to win under caution. The Biff, who was in first when the field was frozen, was awarded the win despite the fact that he failed to get up to speed and both Clint Bowyer and Jimmie Johnson passed him at the finish. After he coasted across the finish line, Biffle's crew pushed his car into Victory Lane.

4. Brett Bodine, North Wilkesboro Speedway (1990). Bodine scored the only win of his NASCAR Sprint Cup Series career at this confusing race, where a caution flag was thrown in the middle of a series of green-flag pit stops. After 18 laps of caution, Dale Earnhardt Sr. was declared the winner. Then the decision was reversed and Bodine, who led 146 laps during the race, was awarded the win.

3. Rusty Wallace barely beats Jeff Gordon (1998). The Budweiser Shootout of 1998 came down to a thrilling last-lap sprint following the second caution of the race. Rusty Wallace took the checkered flag, but Jeff Gordon, who had the most favorable position after the caution, accused Wallace of illegally jumping the restart. Gordon was uncharacteristically vocal about it, too. For his part, Wallace said he followed the rules laid out at the driver's meeting prior to the race. "I wasn't going to wait for him to get a half a car or two cars ahead of me," said Wallace.

2. Bobby Allison's 85th win (1971). On August 6, 1971, at Bowman Gray Stadium in Winston-Salem, North Carolina, Bobby Allison finished first, but the victory was not officially counted by NASCAR because Allison drove a Ford Mustang—a Grand American series car. To this day, the NASCAR Hall of Fame inductee Bobby Allison insists he won that day and lists his total wins at 85 races, not the officially listed 84.

1. Inaugural Daytona 500 (1959). The first run of the Great American Race in 1959 resulted in a photo finish when No. 42 Lee Petty and No. 73 Johnny Beauchamp crossed the finish line together. Officials initially thought Beauchamp was the winner. But Petty protested and NASCAR founder Bill France delayed officially announcing a winner until photos and newsreels could be reviewed. Three days later, Petty was declared champ and was awarded a trophy and a check for $19,050.

"They look like cucumbers with hayraker wheels."
—Joe Weatherly, a NASCAR driver in the 1950s and 1960s, on Indy cars

Back in the day, Bill France Sr. used to invite competitors from the 24-hour race to stay for the Daytona 500, hoping to capitalize on the popularity that open-wheel drivers then enjoyed. But things have changed. Now, promoters of the Rolex 24 recruit the NASCAR guys to run.

A handful of NASCAR drivers have had open-wheel success over the years. Donnie Allison finished fourth in the 1970 Indy 500 and was named Indy 500 Rookie of the Year. During his Rookie of the Year season of 1999, NASCAR Sprint Cup Series driver Tony Stewart competed in both the IndyCar Series' Indy 500 and NASCAR's Coca-Cola 600 in the same day, finishing ninth and fourth respectively. Then he did it again in 2001 with even better results, finishing sixth in the Indy 500 and third at Charlotte. Robbie Gordon has also driven in both races on the same day.

Although people say that drivers are drivers, NASCAR is the top form of motorsports in America today. If you want to race against the best, this is the place to be. Many drivers have attempted to cross over to NASCAR in the last few decades, with mixed results. Here are the ones who have arguably done it with the most success.

10. Ricky Carmichael. It was a big leap from motocross to trucks, but Carmichael, the 15-time American Motorcyclist Association champion, took it and ran with it. In 2010, he made his NASCAR Nationwide Series debut.

9. Danica Patrick. When the only woman in history to lead the Indianapolis 500 and the highest-finishing female in Indy 500 history crossed over to NASCAR, she was already a household name. In 2010, she finished 43rd in points in the NASCAR Nationwide Series and at the Homestead race led the first laps of her NASCAR career. She announced in August 2010 that she planned to run in the NASCAR Nationwide Series fulltime in 2012.

8. Adrian Fernandez. The 1991 Mexican Formula Three Champion and longtime CART, IndyCar, and Le Mans driver made his mark in NASCAR when he drove the Lowe's/Hitachi Power Tools Chevrolet in the first NASCAR Nationwide Series race held outside the United States—at Mexico City's historic Hermanos Rodriguez track in 2005. He ran a total of 10 NASCAR Nationwide races in his NASCAR career, scoring one top 10 finish.

7. Dario Franchitti. The three-time IndyCar Series champion (2007, 2009, and 2010) and two-time Indy 500 winner (2007 and 2010) drove in the NASCAR Camping World Truck Series in 2007 and the NASCAR Nationwide Series in 2007 and 2008, when he won the Coors Light Pole Award at Watkins Glen. In 2009, Franchitti returned to open-wheel driving, but always leaves his options open.

6. Jacques Villeneuve. In the 1990s, Villeneuve won the Indy 500, a CART Series title, and the Formula One championship. In 2007, he made his NASCAR debut in the NASCAR Camping World Truck and the NASCAR Nationwide Series in 2008, marking his best finish (third) at the 2010 NASCAR Nationwide race at the Circuit Gilles Villeneuve, the track named for his father. He ran in a couple NASCAR Nationwide road course races for Penske Racing in 2011, winning the pole in the Montreal race and finishing third at Road America. He's appeared in three NASCAR Sprint Cup races since 2007.

5. Patrick Carpentier. Best known for his career as a Champ Car and IndyCar driver, Carpentier crossed over to NASCAR in 2007, and in 2008, he won the Coors Light Pole Award at the NASCAR Sprint Cup Series race in New Hampshire. He retired in 2011 after competing in the NASCAR Nationwide race at Montreal's Circuit Gilles Villeneuve, a venue where he placed second twice during his NASCAR run. He's appeared in 40 NASCAR Sprint Cup races since 2007.

4. John Andretti. Like several members of his famous family, Andretti made his name in racing as an open-wheel driver. He made his NASCAR debut in 1993, and scored his first of two NASCAR Sprint Cup wins in 1997. In 2007, he pulled a double and drove in the Indy 500 and Coca-Cola 600 on the same day.

3. Juan Pablo Montoya. When he was an open-wheel driver, Juan Pablo Montoya compared stock cars to taxi cabs. But after a six-year career as a Formula One competitor, Montoya hit the NASCAR Sprint Cup Series in 2006. After being named Rookie of the Year in 2007, he dug in for the long haul. He has two career wins, both in road-course events. He's notched 20 top five finishes and 49 top 10 finishes, and had his best points finish (eighth) in 2009.

2. Mario Andretti. As the only driver to win a Daytona 500 (1967), an Indianapolis 500 (1969), and the Formula One championship (1978), Andretti has serious bragging rights. In 1999, the Associated Press named Andretti Driver of the Century over powerhouses A. J. Foyt, Richard Petty, and Dale Earnhardt Sr. Although he only ran 14 NASCAR Sprint Cup races, those credentials still land him at the top of this list . . . almost.

1. A.J. Foyt. Along with rival Mario Andretti, Foyt is one of only two drivers to win both the Daytona 500 and Indy 500. He is the only driver to win the Indy 500 (four times), the Daytona 500, the 24 Hours of Le Mans, and the Rolex 24 at Daytona. Named one of NASCAR's 50 Greatest Drivers, he ran 128 NASCAR Sprint Cup Series races over 30 years, with seven wins and 36 top 10 finishes.

"NASCAR: Everything else is just a game."

Drivers play as hard as they work. Although many drivers also drive go-karts, dune buggies, hot rods, four-wheelers, motorcycles, dirt-track cars, or boats, or pilot their own planes or helicopters on their days off, some drivers manage to occasionally come out from behind the wheel. Here, in no particular order, are some of NASCAR's leading figures and their favorite ways to enjoy their time off.

17. Bill France. Big Bill used to sing and play the ukulele while cruising on his beloved boat, the *Little Kaye*. Often, the musically inclined father of NASCAR would be joined by his friend, country singer and NASCAR driver Marty Robbins.

16. Tony Stewart. He played the trombone in his high school band and still plays bass guitar, but on most of his days off, Smoke can usually be found at his dirt track, Eldora Speedway, in Rossburg, Ohio.

15. Kyle Busch. Lives to drive. If he's not competing in a NASCAR Sprint Cup, NASCAR Camping World Truck, or NASCAR Nationwide Series race, he's racing dune buggies in Nevada, running for the Late Model team he owns, or racing radio-controlled cars.

14. Rick Hendrick. A day off means a day on the water for deep-sea fishing.

13. Richard Childress. Off the track, he's a gun collector and big-game hunter who has bagged Africa's "Dangerous Seven" (a lion, leopard, buffalo, elephant, rhino, hippo, and crocodile).

12. Brian Vickers. Likes skydiving, wakeboarding, and mountain biking. And shopping at Apple (Mac) stores.

11. Carl Edwards. Rides his bike, works on the independent record label he owns, or plays four-hour racquetball tournaments with his childhood friends.

10. Regan Smith. Hits the slopes for snowboarding in Colorado.

9. Jimmy Spencer. Look for him in his garden, fussing over his annuals and perennials.

8. Elliott Sadler. Hunting with his Tennessee Walker hunting dogs or watching sports, especially University of North Carolina basketball games.

7. Kasey Kahne. Boating or wakeboarding on Charlotte's Lake Norman.

6. Ryan Newman. When he's not tinkering with old cars, he goes fishing. Every chance he gets.

5. Jamie McMurray. Addicted to golf.

4. Dale Earnhardt Sr. Loved to hunt and fish. Not surprisingly, he was really intense about it.

3. Jeff Gordon. On race day, he hydrates with pomegranate juice. On days off, he tastes wine, which counts as research for his line of Jeff Gordon chardonnay, merlot, and cabernet sauvignon.

2. Kyle Petty. A lot of drivers ride motorcycles, but KP takes it to a whole other level by leading the annual Kyle Petty Charity Ride, a nine-day, 2400-mile trek that raises money and awareness for his Victory Junction. He also plays pretty good guitar.

1. Bobby Allison. Many drivers and car team owners fly their own planes. But Allison made a sport out of it. He was famous for flipping his plane (and his passengers) upside down during the approach to his home airport in Bessemer, Alabama.

Every win in NASCAR is emotional, because a win is so hard to come by. But here are a few that hit true NASCAR fans right in the gut.

12. Daytona International Speedway (February 2011). It will be impossible to forget the joy on Daytona 500 underdog winner Trevor Bayne's face in Victory Lane, which he located only after asking for directions. Bayne (the youngest driver to ever win the Great American Race) gave the Wood Brothers (the oldest team in NASCAR) their fifth Daytona 500 win, and their first since David Pearson took the checkered flag at Daytona in 1976.

11. Daytona International Speedway (February 2001). Michael Waltrip's first win in about 400 races came on NASCAR's biggest stage, with his brother, Darrell, making the call as a broadcaster.

10. Atlanta Motor Speedway (November 1992). The season finale in 1992 was emotional on several counts: it was Richard Petty's last race as a NASCAR driver; fan favorite Bill Elliott won the race; Alan Kulwicki, an underdog but another big fan favorite, scored enough points to win the NASCAR Sprint Cup Series championship by a mere 10 points; and, while not many people noticed it at the time, a new driver named Jeff Gordon made his NASCAR Sprint Cup debut.

9. Richmond International Raceway (February 1986). So many people were pulling for Kyle Petty when he earned his first career win driving the No. 7 Ford Thunderbird for Wood Brothers Racing. It was a nail-biter in which Petty, who was running fifth, wheeled his way through a last-lap crash to take the checkered flag.

8. Daytona International Speedway (February 1993). Although he made his NASCAR Sprint Cup debut in 1988, Dale Jarrett had only one win to his credit prior to the 1993 Daytona 500. With two laps to go, Jarrett made his move on Dale Earnhardt Sr. and took the checkered flag. His father, Ned, was on the air for CBS, making the call as his son crossed the finish line. The victory marked a turning point for Dale Jarrett, who went on to win 32 more races over the next 12 seasons and capture the 1999 NASCAR Sprint Cup championship.

7. Rockingham (February 2001). Just one week after his car owner and mentor, Dale Earnhardt Sr., had passed away, Steve Park took the checkered flag just ahead of Bobby Labonte. According to Park, the swell of emotion he felt during the final five laps was overwhelming.

6. Daytona International Speedway (February 2010). He'd lost a ride when his former team was forced to shrink from five cars to four. Then he found a deal, but only a one-year deal. Jamie McMurray's future was uncertain, but what a sight it was when he won the Daytona 500 and dropped to his hands and knees. Not a dry eye in Victory Lane.

5. Indianapolis Motor Speedway (August 2005). As a child, Tony Stewart used to peer through the fence at the Brickyard and dream. As he made his final laps to win his first race at his home track, he swears he could pick his father's face out of the crowd. No one could miss the joy on Stewart's face or the elation of his crew as they made their now-famous celebratory fence climb.

4. Charlotte Motor Speedway (May 1994). Jeff Gordon's first NASCAR Sprint Cup Series career win came during the Coca-Cola 600, NASCAR's longest race. Again with the tears.

3. Michigan International Speedway (June 1997). Ernie Irvan's triumphant return to the track where he wrecked three years earlier would have been stirring enough. But then Irvan went and won the race.

2. Daytona International Speedway (July 2001). Just five months after his father died as a result of a crash at Daytona, Dale Earnhardt Jr. crossed the finish line first in what was arguably the most bittersweet win in recent memory. From Victory Lane, Dale Jr. famously said, "My dad was in the passenger seat right with me today."

1. Daytona International Speedway (February 1998). This race tops so many lists, including the fan-voted 50 Greatest Races of All Time. But there's no getting around it. After 19 years of trying, and after winning everything else at this track, and after the frustration of coming so close so many times, Dale Earnhardt Sr. finally won the Daytona 500.

There's a first time for everything. And NASCAR seems to be constantly reinventing itself. Here are some of the most memorable groundbreakers, trailblazers, and first-timers that this sport has seen over the years.

16. Brickyard Debut. In 1994, NASCAR ran its first race at the famous home of the Indianapolis 500, kicking off an annual Brickyard tradition.

15. You Like Me. In May 2011, Talladega Superspeedway became the first NASCAR track to claim more than 100,000 "likes" on Facebook.

14. Homesteader. The first winner at the brand-new Homestead-Miami Speedway in 1999 was Tony Stewart. His win capped off a record year in which he won three races as a rookie.

13. Starting Line. On July 18, 1958, at Toronto's Canadian National Exposition Speedway, a 21-year-old named Richard Petty made his first-ever NASCAR Sprint Cup Series start in what was then the NASCAR Grand National Division. He finished 17th in a field of 19 after he hit the fence on the 55th lap.

12. Let There Be Light. During the 1991 NASCAR Sprint All-Star Race at Charlotte Motor Speedway, cars raced under artificial lights for the first time. This was track president Humpy Wheeler's baby. And it was an incredible sight.

11. Lucky 13. In 1975, Richard Petty set a modern-era record when he became the first driver with 13 wins in a season. Then Jeff Gordon tied the record in 1998.

10. Bump Drafting. It's said that Junior Johnson accidentally discovered drafting during a practice session prior to the 1960 Daytona 500, when he slipped into the airspace behind a faster car. He put his discovery from practice into action during the actual race and won it.

9. Family Business. The Pettys were the first family to actually make a living in racing. They did it mostly by sticking together. In 1967, when Richard Petty broke his father Lee's record of 54 victories to become NASCAR's all-time winningest driver, he refused to disrespect his dad. "There's been a lot of fuss lately over me tying or breaking Daddy's record of 54 victories," said the King. "We never thought of it that way. As far as we're concerned, the Petty family has 109 wins."

8. Star Power. Glenn "Fireball" Roberts, the 1962 Daytona 500 winner who got his nickname courtesy of the lightning fastball he threw as a Florida State baseball player, was arguably NASCAR's first superstar.

7. Race Restriction. In 1988, NASCAR sought to temper the ever-accelerating speeds being hit at superspeedways by instituting restrictor-plate racing at Daytona and Talladega. Soon after, average race speeds dropped from the 170s to the 150s and lower.

6. For Life. When Scientifically Treated Petroleum, better known as STP, signed a lifetime deal with Richard Petty in 1972, it became the first national sponsor in NASCAR Sprint Cup Series racing and set the standard for all future sponsorships.

5. Then There Were Four. In 2007, Toyota joined NASCAR's Big Three car companies by entering into race competition. The next year, Kyle Busch won the first race for Toyota at Atlanta Motor Speedway, scoring the first victory for a foreign car at the NASCAR Sprint Cup Series level since 1954, when Al Keller won with a Jaguar in NASCAR's first road-course race in Linden, New Jersey.

4. Million Dollar Bill. Not only was he NASCAR's most popular driver at the time, but in 1985, Bill Elliott also became the first driver to win a $1 million bonus.

3. Three-Peat. Cale Yarborough set a mark when he won an unprecedented three straight NASCAR Sprint Cup Series championships in 1976, 1977, and 1978.

2. Four . . . No, Five-Peat. In 2009, Jimmie Johnson became the first driver to win four NASCAR Sprint Cup championships in a row. Then, incredibly, he became the five-peat champ the following year. In doing so, he scored another first when he became the first driver in the seven-year history of the Chase for the NASCAR Sprint Cup to overcome a points deficit in the season finale to win the championship.

1. Barrier Breaker. Buddy Baker was the first driver to break the 200-mph mark on a superspeedway when he ran 200.447 mph on March 24, 1970, at Talladega.

It's an accepted fact that NASCAR fans rival all others in terms of enthusiasm and dedication. Nowhere is that more evident than in the race track infield, where fans often turn a one- or two-day event into a three-day or four-day extravaganza. Because fans can only spend so many hours cooking restrictor-plate chili from Mario Batali's *Mario Tailgates NASCAR Style* cookbook, sometimes they need to find other things to do. Here are some of the best ways fans have been known to pass the time before the green flag waves.

10. Horseshoes. At Texas Motor Speedway, everything is supersized—including the big-as-a-football-field tailgater's pit stop park, complete with horseshoe pits and beanbag toss areas. In Texas, tailgaters even have their own magazine, *Tailgater Monthly*.

9. Juggling. At Pocono, they send in the clowns.

8. Vetting frustration. At Watkins Glen International (and several other tracks), fans can kick, punch, or pose with life-size plywood cut-outs of the starting grid (Jeff Gordon, Kyle Busch, Tony Stewart, etc.) courtesy of the "Fathead Guy," a fan who sets up a cluster of driver likenesses in the infield.

7. Doppelgangers. Inspired by a similar competition in nearby Key West, fans stage an impromptu Ernest Hemingway look-alike contest at Homestead-Miami Speedway.

6. Construction. At Texas Motor Speedway, fans spent hours building scaffolding three stories high so they could see the race from their position on the infield.

5. Sing-along. Prior to the Bristol race in 2009, some 160,000 fans broke the *Guinness Book of World Records* mark for "Largest Group Karaoke" when they sang "Friends in Low Places" by Garth Brooks.

4. Bob's party bus. In the late 1990s, a former Indiana school bus with an abstract-expressionist Jackson Pollock paint scheme began appearing regularly at Michigan International Speedway. When the original owner passed away, a fan named Kevin Kent bought the bus and kept the party torch lit. The bus still makes the rounds, notably at Talladega, but Kent found Jesus in 2007, so these days it's more "praise the Lord" than "party central." Just look for the 30-foot cross, decorated with multicolored Christmas lights.

3. Improvisation. During one particularly rainy race weekend at Talladega, many vehicles and motor homes got stuck in the mud. One camper was submerged in water, but a group of fans set up chairs and coolers on its roof and kept the party going.

2. Initiation. At Michigan International Speedway, it's a tradition for fans visiting the infield for the first time to wear a rookie stripe (yellow police tape on their bodies) similar to the yellow rookie stripe that first-time NASCAR Sprint Cup Series drivers are required to display on their back bumper.

1. I do. Ever since 2002, couples have been invited to take their wedding vows prior to the race at Bristol Motor Speedway. Other tracks, including Darlington and Richmond, also organize weddings, but Bristol may have taken the cake when one year, 24 couples from 11 states gathered at the start/finish line for their nuptials. They all signed their marriage paperwork with markers provided by the race sponsor, Sharpie. The brides were also given Sharpie marker bouquets.

Besides race tracks, there are other famous NASCAR landmarks well worth the pilgrimage. Here are some favorites.

10. North Carolina State Fairgrounds, Raleigh, North Carolina. In 2010, the governor of North Carolina, Bev Perdue, along with Junior Johnson, unveiled a marker to commemorate the historic half-mile dirt track where so many of the sport's legends got their start. Johnson led the track's first NASCAR-sanctioned race in 1955 until it was called off due to rain. Richard Petty won the final NASCAR race at the track in 1970. The back straightaway was converted into a parking lot in the 1990s, although the venue still hosts events such as demolition derbies and tractor pulls.

9. Racing's North Turn, Ponce Inlet, Florida. This restaurant, chock full of racing photos and memorabilia, is located on Highway A1A, in the location where Daytona's former road course began.

8. The Streamline Hotel, Daytona Beach, Florida. In December 1947, Bill France gathered promoters from around the country for a meeting at the hotel located on Highway A1A to form the organization that would become NASCAR. The hotel still stands.

7. Wood Brothers Racing Museum, Stuart, Virginia. Although the oldest continuously operating team in NASCAR moved its race shop to Harrisburg, North Carolina, the museum has all the goodies, including a replica of Glen Wood's original 1940s backseat racer.

6. International Motorsports Hall of Fame, Talladega, Alabama. A museum located next to the track at Talladega and dedicated to all things motorsports. Very cool artifacts from the fastest boat in the world to the Budweiser Rocket Car.

5. The beach, Daytona Beach, Florida. The beach where the first beach-course races were run in the 1930s is still as big and wide and flat as it was in NASCAR's early days. Although they no longer race there, cars are still allowed to drive and park right on the beach.

4. National Motorsports Press Association (NMPA) Stock Car Hall of Fame – Joe Weatherly Museum, Darlington, South Carolina. On the grounds of Darlington Raceway, motorheads will drool over the display of illegal car engine parts.

3. Victory Junction, Randleman, North Carolina. Opened in 2004 by Kyle and Pattie Petty in honor of their son, Adam, Victory Junction is a colorful, vibrant, energetic camp for seriously ill children. If you haven't seen this incredible place, which offers tours, you should.

2. Dale Earnhardt, Inc. (DEI), Mooresville, North Carolina. The 24,000-square-foot facility is more than just the corporate headquarters of DEI. The vast showroom and museum, complete with all seven of Earnhardt's championship trophies and other memorabilia, is a must-see for diehard Intimidator fans. Earnhardt's hometown of Kannapolis, which is just down the road, offers a self-guided tour on the Dale Trail, a path that ends up in Dale Earnhardt Plaza. Just look for the nine-foot bronze statue of Earnhardt.

1. NASCAR Hall of Fame, Charlotte, North Carolina. The building is impressive, interactive and most importantly, it's fun. Not many museums let visitors actually perform a television broadcast or simulate an actual race. The NASCAR Hall of Fame is a gleaming tribute to the sport of stock car racing packed with artifacts (from David Pearson's No. 21 car to Jeff Gordon's first helmet) that define NASCAR's history.

It's not all about luck. When they say a driver got lucky and won a race, keep in mind that he was in the position to win, and it wasn't luck that got him close. Here are the drivers who most memorably seized their lucky opportunities.

6. Luck Fit for a King. During the 1981 running of the Great American Race, all eyes were on Bobby Allison, who was the fastest qualifier, had the fastest car in practice, and led close to half of the race's 200 laps. But with just 26 laps remaining, Allison's luck ran out when he ran out of gas and was forced to sputter to the pits on fumes. The King, so often "lucky" enough to be in the hunt for victory, seized the lead and kept it for his record seventh Daytona 500 win.

5. No. 17. Next to Dale Earnhardt Sr., Darrell Waltrip had the most famous unlucky Daytona 500 streak. After running and losing the race 16 times, Waltrip turned his luck around when, at the end of the 1989 race, he rolled the dice and beat the leaders on fuel mileage.

4. Born Lucky. It's often said that second-generation drivers of NASCAR's biggest stars—such as Kyle Petty and Dale Earnhardt Jr.—were born lucky. No denying that. But there's another point of view. As lucky as these drivers have been to get the opportunities they might not have gotten if their last names had been something different, they are under constant pressure and scrutiny that other lesser-known drivers are lucky enough to skip.

3. Free Pass. In 2003, with the goal of increased safety, NASCAR banned racing back to the yellow following a caution. This new rule is nicknamed "Free Pass" because under this provision, the first driver one lap down automatically gets his lap back when the caution comes out, with a few caveats, including making the rule null and void during the last 10 laps of the race. The first driver to benefit from the rule was Ryan Newman at the 2003 Dover race. He not only got his free pass, he went on to win the race.

2. Golden Horseshoe. People often talk about the good luck of five-time NASCAR Sprint Cup Series champion Jimmie Johnson. But is it luck when Johnson time and again finds himself in the right spot to pounce the moment someone else sputters? Probably not.

1. Lucky Charm. On his 20th try, Dale Earnhardt Sr. finally won the 1998 Daytona 500, which many count as the biggest win of his career. Earnhardt later disclosed that prior to the race, a young girl named Wessa Miller had given him a good-luck penny, which the Intimidator glued to his dashboard. Perhaps luckiest of all were the fans who were fortunate enough to attend the 1998 Daytona 500 and witness that piece of NASCAR history in-person.

NASCAR has more of the top 20 highest-attended sporting events in the U.S. than any other sport. The big events attract fans from all over the country and the world. When you put nearly 200,000 people in one place for one event, you're going to see some odd things. Here are a few classics.

7. Feathers Flying. During qualifying for the NASCAR Nationwide Series race at Daytona in 2003, Michael Waltrip hit a seagull. Mikey said he felt bad about it, but gathered his sense of humor in time for his appearance on *Trackside*, where he began his interview by unleashing a fistful of feathers.

6. Fan on the Track. The fan, who was apparently intoxicated, ran across the Pocono track during the 1993 race, and then managed to scale the wall mere seconds before the cars driven by Davey Allison and Kyle Petty sped past. Authorities apprehended the man in a swamp near the track and held him on a $20,000 bond.

5. Autograph Request. During a red flag at Watkins Glen in 2007, a fan climbed a fence, walked onto the track and approached Matt Kenseth's car. The fan then reached through the passenger side window and asked Kenseth to sign his hat. Kenseth replied, "I'm a little busy right now."

Greg Biffle was heard saying to Kenseth over the car radio, "Wouldn't it have been nice if he was bringing you some brakes?"

The fan was immediately apprehended and arrested. No word if he ever got Kenseth to sign his hat.

4. The King Keeps His Cool. While being treated for an on-track injury, Richard Petty was at once surprised and a little miffed when one of the paramedics attending to him asked for his autograph. True to form, the King obliged.

3. Holler uncle. Years ago, at North Carolina's historic North Wilkesboro Speedway, a fan threw a jar of white liquor over the fence and onto the track. It landed right in front of a driver who was, at the time, giving hometown favorite Junior Johnson a run for his money. The fan, who was escorted off the premises by authorities, turned out to be Johnson's uncle, Ernest Money.

2. Wildlife on the Track. Because Pocono Raceway sits in the mountains surrounded by acres of woods, it's not surprising that over the years there have been dozens of caution flags waved due to ducks, geese, or deer jumping, running, walking, or flying onto the track during a race.

Before the days of two-way radio communication, the Pocono flagman had a special "deer on the track" hand signal (he'd hold up four fingers over his head to represent antlers). Neil Bonnett once actually hit a deer during a race after the deer jumped in front of his car between Turn 2 and Turn 3.

1. Funeral Procession. At the Hickory Motor Speedway in Hickory, North Carolina, races would be stopped whenever the adjacent Catawba Memorial Gardens cemetery held a funeral service. Drivers, crews, track personnel, the media, and fans were all notified ahead of time to expect the red flag. After the funeral procession made its way to the burial site and the service was complete, the race would resume.

Mechanics and car builders in NASCAR are always on the lookout for a slight edge. They work their magic, and then sometimes hold their breath when NASCAR inspectors come to take a look under the hood. Over the years, a few cars have famously pushed the rule-book envelope. Here are some we won't soon forget.

10. Backseat Driver. In the 1950s and 1960s, the Wood Brothers took the more liberal rules for modified cars to the limit when Leonard Wood decided to move the engine and the driver rearward—with the driver ending up in the backseat—in their 1937 Ford with a 1958 Edsel engine. The "backseat car" was virtually unbeatable on Virginia and North Carolina short tracks with 2012 NASCAR Hall of Fame Inductee Glen Wood driving it.

9. Where There's Smoke. The legendary car owner/mechanic Smokey Yunick was known to put his creativity to work back in the day. In the 1960s, Yunick was nabbed building a 7/8th-scale car. Officials grew suspicious when his cars ran 1/8th faster than the rest of the field.

8. Beach Modification. After placing first in the 1955 Daytona Beach race, Fireball Roberts was stripped of his win after a post-race inspection revealed an illegal engine modification. NASCAR gave Tim Flock the win. This was the last time a driver's win was taken away for an engine violation.

7. King's Ransom. In 1983, Richard Petty was fined $38,000 for an oversized engine in his famous Plymouth.

6. Junior's Last Stand. In 1995, just before he retired as a car owner, Junior Johnson was fined a then-record $45,000 for an illegal intake manifold in Brett Bodine's car at Daytona. Even though the car didn't look outrageous on the outside, according to NASCAR's rules, any internal modification to a car's engine must be visibly welded in place and this one wasn't. Crew chief Mike Beam was also fined $100 and placed on indefinite probation.

5. Bill Elliott's Thunderbird. In 1987, Elliott set the record for fastest qualifying in his famous No. 9 Ford that many considered to be a slightly shrunken version of his competitors' cars. He set a mark at Daytona (210.364) then topped it at Talladega (212.809) in a car that passed NASCAR inspection by a nose.

4. Illicit Lift. At Talladega in 1995, driver Ricky Rudd and manager Bill Ingle were fined $45,000 for illegally installing a hydraulic lift under the rear deck lid of Rudd's car. Ingenious, but blatant.

3. Puff Daddy. Chad Knaus is not the only crew chief who has fielded controversial cars over the years. But when you win a lot, the microscope comes out.

Following Jimmie Johnson's 2006 Daytona 500 qualifying run, Knaus was suspended (for Daytona and three subsequent races) and fined $25,000 after an inspection determined that the rear window of Johnson's car had been altered to change its aerodynamics. Johnson, whose crew immediately rebuilt the car (which passed three inspections), went on to win the race.

In 2007, Knaus was again fined—this time for a record $100,000—and suspended for six races when officials questioned the shape of the fenders on two Hendrick cars (the No. 24 and the No. 48) prior to the road-race debut of the new car design. The message? Don't mess with the new car.

2. The Yellow Banana. Junior Johnson, who was well-known for pushing the limits of the NASCAR rule book, built one of the most controversial cars of all time for Fred Lorenzen to drive in Atlanta in 1966. The Ford Galaxy, with a chopped-off roof and a sloping body covered by a bright yellow Holly Farms paint scheme, earned the nickname, "The Yellow Banana." NASCAR allowed it, mostly in an attempt to lure back Ford, which had been absent from the sport for years.

1. T-Rex. Jeff Gordon's 1997 NASCAR Sprint All-Star Race-winning ride bent every rule in the NASCAR book. Nicknamed "T-Rex" for its *The Lost World: Jurassic Park* movie paint scheme and for owner Rick Evernham's engineer, Rex Stump, the car had been "optimized" in its every detail—from the bigger frame rails to the relocated suspension system elements. Gordon said the car, where everything was slightly raised, stuck to the track like nothing he'd ever felt before.

Although T-Rex was declared legal for the All-Star race, NASCAR soon rewrote the rule book specifically to turn this car into a dinosaur. It made only one more appearance at Indianapolis, in a highly altered state. Although the legend remains, T-Rex remains extinct.

This really could be a list of just people named France. From the foresight of Bill Sr. to the hard work of Bill Jr. and Betty Jane, the Frances created NASCAR and developed it into what it looks like it today. But here are some others who helped shape the sport along the way.

10. Pioneering drivers of the 1940s. They blazed a trail for all future drivers by improvising everything from driving styles to "safety belts" (tying themselves in with ropes or wearing truck inner tubes around their waists).

9. Wood Brothers. Brought us some of the best drivers and revolutionized the pit stop.

8. Wendell Scott. Broke down barriers in the 1960s as the first—and, for most of his career, the only—African-American driver in NASCAR Sprint Cup Series competition.

7. Janet Guthrie. As the first woman to compete in both the Daytona 500 and the Indy 500, she showed the world that a driver is a driver.

6. Alan Kulwicki. Brought engineering to the forefront of the sport.

5. Rick Hendrick. Took the multicar team concept and worked it for 10 championships.

4. Ray Evernham. Revolutionized the crew chief position and defined the NASCAR work ethic.

3. Jeff Gordon. Made winning look easy. And continues to do so.

2. Dale Earnhardt Sr. Epitomized the title of "NASCAR Champion."

1. Richard Petty. Defined how a driver should act on and off the track.

Intimidation: Dale Earnhardt Sr.'s and Rusty Wallace's Best Practical Jokes by Kenny Wallace

Kenny Wallace burst onto the NASCAR scene in 1988. The following year, 1989, he won the NASCAR Nationwide Series Rookie of the Year Award. The following season, 1990, he debuted in the NASCAR Sprint Cup Series, where he has gone on to claim three Coors Light Pole Awards and notch more than two dozen top 10 finishes. Wallace has also earned nine wins and 170 top 10 finishes in the NASCAR Nationwide Series, where he's been named Most Popular Driver of the Year three times.

The son of a prominent race car driver, younger brother to two others, and uncle to two more, Kenny Wallace has not only followed in the Wallace family tradition of becoming a successful driver, he has also established himself as an on-air commentator for SPEED's *NASCAR RaceDay* and *NASCAR Victory Lane*. Through it all, Wallace has remained one of the sport's most intriguing personalities and jokers— someone who knows all too well that when you put a lot of people in a confined space for a long period of time, it's inevitable—there will be practical jokes played. (Which begs the question: why are they called practical? They're usually anything but sensible or useful.)

Pranks in NASCAR are traditional, and some are legendary. Sterling Marlin's been known to throw sticks of dynamite in occupied rental cars or bathroom stalls. (Imagine the sight of big crewmen running out of the men's room with a terrified look on his face.) Tony Stewart and Greg Biffle once hovered around the corner at the track in Texas, giggling like little kids as they watched Carl Edwards try to untie his mountain bike, which they had fastened to a pole with dozens of zip ties. And once, Neil Bonnett convinced a little boy to run up and hug David Pearson as he left a crowded restaurant and holler, "Daddy! Daddy!"

But possibly NASCAR's best-known prankster was Dale Earnhardt Sr. Here, Kenny Wallace—who along with his brother, Rusty Wallace, was on the receiving end of several of Earnhardt's pranks over the years—shares some classic Intimidator give-and-take.

Honorable Mention. This has nothing to do with Dale Earnhardt, but the second-best practical joker I ever saw was Harry Benfield, a NASCAR legend who worked for Junior Johnson. He was known for putting ex-lax in people's food and things like that. But once, in 1984, when I was working as the crew chief on the Levi Garrett team, I saw his best work.

Everybody was just sitting around. I looked down in the garage area and saw him get a tractor-trailer tire inner tube and put it underneath the car where his friend, Shorty, was sleeping. Then he hooked the inner tube to an air hose and started blowing it up. It was so strong it lifted the whole car off the ground. Finally, that thing blew up and that guy about had a heart attack! This was back when we had no motor homes—or cell phones—so you had to be creative.

8. Pink slip. When I was around 26 years old, I was building a go-kart track behind my house for fun. I told Dale about it and mentioned that I needed a water tank to water the track. My wife calls me one day when I'm out of town and says, "Dale Earnhardt and his friend just showed up." They showed up and pushed an old water truck onto our property and said, "Here, this is for Kenny."

So, I cut this big tank off the truck, situate it, and fill it with water. As I filled it, all the water came draining out; it had a thousand itty-bitty holes in it.

The next week I saw Dale's wife, Teresa, and she said, "We forgot to give you the title to the truck." We all laughed about it. Then later I took it to the scrap yard. They said, "We can't take this. It's too rusted out." I had to pay someone to take it; I couldn't give it away.

7. Something fishy. Earnhardt and my brother, Rusty, had been going at it pretty hard, week after week. Then one day, Rusty got in his car at Darlington on a 100-degree day, gets all strapped in and says, "Oh my God, it stinks so bad!" Dale had put an open can of sardines under Rusty's seat. Rusty had to drive with them under his seat all day.

6. No wheel left behind. The next week, to get even, Rusty stole Earnhardt's steering wheel right before the start of the race. Earnhardt high-fived everyone, jumped in his car and started freaking out. Rusty was holding the steering wheel outside the window.

5. Nifty fifty. Rusty was asking for serious retaliation—if you played a joke on Dale, he'd pay you back double time—but once, Rusty taped a $50 bill to the roof of Dale's car. It's an old superstition in NASCAR that fifties are bad luck. Rusty said Dale jumped out of the car like he'd seen a snake!

4. Toil and trouble. Again, Rusty was risking payback, but another time, his crew guys had a guy stand in front of Dale's car before a race in North Wilkesboro and chant as if he was putting a hex on the car. Dale did not like that!

3. Timber! Our SPEED channel colleague Steve Byrnes was filming Earnhardt working on his farm years ago when Earnhardt revved up the engine on his bulldozer, purposely plowed into a tree and knocked it over. It barely missed Steve.

2. Artwork. Once, Ricky Rudd had just climbed into his race car, ready to start his engine. When he reached for his goggles, a brand new pair straight out of the box, he noticed two eyeballs drawn on the lenses with marker. He couldn't see a thing. That was Dale's work.

1. Take a dip. The country singer Kix Brooks (of Brooks & Dunn fame)—who, by the way, looks just like Dale—told a story at the Dale Earnhardt Tribute Concert in 2003 about the time the two of them went deep-sea fishing. Brooks had just caught his first marlin and while he was leaning over the side of the boat, Earnhardt grabbed him by the shorts and threw him in the water. Then he took off and left Kix bobbing in the water. He came back, but it took awhile. Then he turned around and sent Kix a huge marlin mount in the mail as a gift. That was so Dale.

The one thing we have no control over is the thing that controls the sport the most—the weather. Specifically, the rain. Because NASCAR Sprint Cup Series cars don't have windshield wipers and run on tires with no treads (a.k.a. "slick tires"), they can't run on a wet track. So when it starts to drizzle, the caution flag goes up. When it starts to rain, the race is red-flagged until the rain stops and the track is completely dry.

If the rain doesn't stop and the halfway point of the race isn't reached when the red flag is thrown, then the race is rescheduled for the next possible date. If the halfway point is reached, then the driver who is leading the race when it is stopped is declared the winner. Here are some of the most memorable rainout wins.

6. Daytona 500s. The Daytona 500 always makes for a memorable win, no matter what the circumstances. The race has been shortened by rain four times since the inaugural race in 1959. In 1965, Fred Lorenzen won after running just 133 laps for 332.5 miles; Richard Petty won in 1966 after running 198 laps for 495 miles; in 2003, Michael Waltrip drove 109 laps for 272.5 miles to get the win; and Matt Kenseth ran 152 laps for 380 miles, which was enough to earn him the 2009 victory.

5. Charlotte Motor Speedway (2009). After it was postponed due to rain on Sunday, the longest race on the NASCAR Sprint Cup circuit was run the next day. Then the rain came again. When the race was red-flagged at Lap 227, David Reutimann, who decided not to pit a few laps prior figuring he had nothing to lose, found himself in the right place at the right time and won the race. It was his first win in 75 career starts and gave Michael Waltrip his first win as a team owner. It was also Reutimann's first appearance on Speed's *NASCAR Victory Lane*, which was taped indoors that day.

4. New Hampshire Motor Speedway (2009). When he won the race after it was stopped following Lap 273, then-rookie Joey Logano not only scored his first-ever NASCAR Sprint Cup race victory, but at 19 years, one month and four days old, he also became the youngest winner in NASCAR Sprint Cup history.

3. Qualifying Rainouts (2008). In 2008, a total of 10 qualifying sessions were rained out, the most ever in one year.

2. Texas Doubleheader (2010). When both the NASCAR Nationwide and NASCAR Sprint Cup races were postponed due to April showers in Texas, the races were run back-to-back on the following Monday, a scenario that rarely gets played out. Fifteen drivers competed in both races, which meant those who finished both clocked a total of 801 miles that day. Denny Hamlin won the NASCAR Sprint Cup race, with Kyle Busch placing third, and then taking the checkered flag at the NASCAR Nationwide race.

1. Rain Man. For a season or two, Jeff Burton was known as the rainout king after he gathered two rainout victories at Darlington in 1999, then another at Las Vegas in 2000. Two of the three races earned Burton (and a lucky fan) a $1 million bonus as part of a sponsor promotion.

Best Track Snacks by Elliott and Hermie Sadler

You wouldn't necessarily know it by looking at him, but Elliott Sadler is always hungry. He must be. Otherwise the Virginian—who has nine wins and 136 top 10 finishes in NASCAR Sprint Cup, NASCAR Nationwide, and NASCAR Camping World Truck Series races—wouldn't have once devoured over a dozen Martinsville hot dogs at Martinsville Speedway or on another occasion eaten 16 South Boston bologna burgers prior to a race at South Boston Speedway in honor of his brother, Hermie, the 1993 NASCAR Nationwide Series Rookie of the Year turned pit reporter for SPEED, who was driving the No. 16 car at the time.

Hermie has a decent appetite as well, enough so to inspire the brothers to open a restaurant, Fosho, in their hometown of Emporia, Virginia.

Now that we've established their credentials as experts on track snacks, here are Elliott and Hermie's picks for the best food found at NASCAR race tracks.

10. Anything from Wolfgang Puck's Apex (Auto Club Speedway).
Preferably the crab cakes and penne pasta.

9. Hot chili peppers and eggs (Phoenix International Raceway). As if it's not hot enough.

8. Venison and quail (Pocono Raceway). Spotted on the grills of tailgating fans.

7. Fried apple pie and frozen cider (Charlotte Motor Speedway). Not sold as a combo, but should be.

6. She-crab soup (Dover International Speedway). When in Dover . . .

5. Chicken spiedini (Kansas Speedway). A ball of chicken meat and cheese served in olive oil. Better than it sounds.

4. Giant turkey legs (Atlanta Motor Speedway). Something to be thankful for.

3. Pork–fried nachos (Texas Motor Speedway). Nachos layered with tender roast pork, melted cheese, pico de gallo, and sour cream. 'Nuff said.

2. South Boston bologna burgers (South Boston Speedway). Why have these not caught on nationwide?

1. Martinsville hot dogs (Martinsville Speedway). Famous for a reason. Prior to every race, food prep workers at the track chop some 1,500 pounds of fresh onions for the dogs. The Sadlers prefer theirs with onions and chili.

The first "live coverage" of NASCAR races came courtesy of local radio stations broadcasting races, such as the first Southern 500 at Darlington in 1950. In the 1960s, many races were broadcast on radio and a few were even shown on TV, with coverage breaking out in the late 1970s and 1980s, and then exploding in the 1990s, along with the sport's popularity.

Today, with more than 150 hours of race coverage per year, NASCAR is the second highest-rated regular sport on television in the United States. Every national series race is carried on TV, with an average of nearly six million viewers watching each NASCAR Sprint Cup Series race.

Here are some favorite NASCAR-on-TV moments from over the years

10. Race Rundown. In 1961, *ABC's Wide World of Sports* began showing race highlights. For many years, this was quite a few sports fans' only exposure to NASCAR.

9. Flag-to-Flag. The first complete telecast of a NASCAR race featured the 1971 event at Greenville Pickens Speedway on ABC. The race was actually taped and shown a full week later, with announcers reading from a script.

8. Snow Day. In 1979, CBS aired the Daytona 500 live. This was the first time a NASCAR race was carried live, in its entirety, on TV. Normally, for a program like this, a few million viewers would tune into CBS—one of only a handful of networks operating at the time. (No cable TV yet!) But the audience on this day was huge, due mostly to a gigantic snowstorm keeping people indoors across all of the Eastern seaboard and a good part of the Midwest. When the captive audience was treated to an exciting race that included a Richard Petty win and the infamous on-track fight between Cale Yarborough and Bobby and Donnie Allison, an untold number of NASCAR fans were born.

7. Close-Up. Also in 1979, TV coverage was upgraded when in-car cameras were introduced. Since then, dozens of improvements have been introduced, including in-car brake cams and foot cams, as well as mini-cams and microphones embedded in the tracks. Today, somewhere between 60 and 70 cameras are used on and around various parts of the track to cover each race.

6. 24-7. In 1981, a new 24-hour sports network called ESPN ran live coverage of the race at Atlanta Motor Speedway.

5. A star is Born. In the early 1990s, ESPN produced a show called *Thursday Night Thunder*, which ran features on various racing series, including midget and sprint cars. One memorable episode featured young midget-series champion Jeff Gordon driving a stock car at Buck Baker's driving school in Rockingham, North Carolina. This was the first time Gordon ever drove a stock car and he was hooked.

4. Daytona 500 (1993). Dale Earnhardt Sr. was the favorite, but another Dale— Dale Jarrett—won it. Calling the race for CBS was a former champion turned broadcaster, Ned Jarrett, who famously shelved his objectivity when he was overcome with excitement for his son on the last lap and urged, "Come on Dale, go, baby, go."

3. Big Bucks. When NASCAR struck a $2.25 billion deal with FOX Sports, FX, NBC, and TNT for national TV rights beginning in 2001, racing hit the big time.

2. All Motorsports, All the Time. In 2002, Speedvision, originally located in Connecticut, was relaunched as the SPEED channel out of Charlotte, North Carolina. Since that time, SPEED has grown into the premier motorsports network and is watched in more than 80 million households.

1. Monkey Moment. It's impossible to pick a favorite moment on *NASCAR Race-Day*, but the show at the June 2008 New Hampshire race stands alone. While running a feature on co-host Jimmy Spencer and his days in the NASCAR Modified Tour, the satellite failed and the show was knocked off the air for more than a half hour. When the feed finally returned, the first thing the audience at home heard was screaming from the live audience reacting to a monkey standing on the shoulder of a guy in the front row. The monkey, who was wearing a diaper, was watching the show while drinking a can of beer.

There are 42 drivers in every race who do not win and some drivers go hundreds of races without winning. So if you win one, you deserve to celebrate. From the standard burnouts and doughnuts to full-on backflips, some celebrations have been more memorable than others. Here are the best of the best.

11. Gordon's No. 3 Flag. When Jeff Gordon surpassed Dale Earnhardt Sr. on the all-time wins list, he took a lap around the track at Phoenix International Raceway with a No. 3 flag hanging out the window. His crew had carried it around for weeks. Another class move by Gordon.

10. Terry Labonte's Smokin' of Victory Lane. After a last-lap tap by Dale Earnhardt Sr. at the 1995 Bristol race, Labonte wrecked but managed to finish first anyway. He sputtered his still-smoking, crunched car into Victory Lane, leaned out of his window and said, "That was a finish, wasn't it?"

9. Kyle Busch's Bow. Busch's trademark gentlemanly bow is how he answers the booing crowd from Victory Lane. Much to his detractors' dismay, he has the opportunity to do it a lot.

8. Mikey's Pop(s). When Michael Waltrip won at Talladega in 2003, he popped out of the escape hatch. Classic Mikey. After a NASCAR Nationwide Series race win 10 years earlier, he popped the question to his girlfriend, Buffy.

7. DW's Dance. After winning the 1989 Daytona 500, Darrell Waltrip celebrated with his best impersonation of the Ickey Shuffle, a dance made famous by Cincinnati Bengals fullback Elbert "Ickey" Woods. Silly, but unforgettable.

6. Dale's Doughnuts. When the Intimidator finally won the Daytona 500 in 1998, he drove slowly down pit road for high-fives and handshakes from virtually every guy in every crew, and then celebrated by doing doughnuts in the infield grass, leaving marks that witnesses say were in the shape of a "3." A few fans took chunks of the beaten-up grass and stuck them into their pockets or coolers while some savored the moment by lying down in the deep ruts.

5. Kurt Busch's Snow Angel. After a win at Bristol in March 2006, Busch hopped out of his car and made a snow angel on the track despite the fact that there was no snow. Busch was commenting on the cancellation of events due to snow the previous day.

4. Tony's Climb. Inspired by Indy 500 champ Helio Castroneves, Tony Stewart and his crew celebrated by climbing the infield fence after winning several races, most memorably after taking the 2007 Brickyard. Later, Stewart kissed the famous bricks, as well as Miss Sprint Cup.

3. Carl Edwards's Backflip. He introduced this celebratory move during his dirt-track days. Ever since, "Edwards" and "backflip" have gone hand in hand in Victory Lane.

2. Kyle Busch Who? Many people were outraged when Busch went rogue rock star and smashed the hand-painted vintage guitar trophy in Victory Lane following his winning the NASCAR Nationwide Series race at Nashville Superspeedway. Busch said he did it to break up the trophy and share the pieces with his crew. Artist Sam Bass said he wished he hadn't spent so many hours painting the one-of-a-kind instrument.

1. Alan Kulwicki's Polish Victory Lap. The 1992 NASCAR Sprint Cup Series champ took his first wrong-way trip around the track in 1988. The wins kept coming and Kulwicki made it his signature move. Many drivers still pay tribute to him by taking a backwards victory lap.

Heartbreak. Misfortune. Disaster. Adversity. Buzzard's luck. Call it what you will. Every driver has a day where things fail to go his way. Here are some of the most memorable hard-luck moments in NASCAR history.

11. Kurt Busch, Richmond International Raceway (2004). At the 2004 Richmond race, Kurt Busch ran out of gas with just eight laps to go, handing Jeremy Mayfield his fourth all-time win and a spot in that year's Chase for the NASCAR Sprint Cup.

10. Jeff Gordon, Charlotte Motor Speedway (1998). As the checkered flag was about to wave at the NASCAR Sprint All-Star Race, Gordon lost the win when he ran out of gas.

9. J.D. McDuffie, everywhere (all the time). Blame it on bad luck. Driver J.D. McDuffie holds the record for most all-time NASCAR Sprint Cup Series race starts with no wins.

8. Dale Earnhardt Jr., Charlotte (2011). The fans were on their feet as Dale Jr. looked poised to win the 2011 Coca-Cola 600. Then came the heavy sigh heard around the racing world when Junior sputtered to a stop, out of fuel, and Kevin Harvick zipped by him for the win.

7. Joey Logano, Phoenix (2011). After breaking a wheel at Bristol earlier in the season, Logano lost an engine at Phoenix, where he ultimately finished in 33rd place.

6. Tony Stewart, Charlotte Motor Speedway (2008). With just three laps to go in the Coca-Cola 600, Tony Stewart cut a tire and handed the win to Kasey Kahne.

5. Jerry Nadeau, Infineon Raceway (2002). Nadeau was leading the race at Sonoma and sniffing his second career NASCAR Sprint Cup win when his transmission broke during the final three laps, opening the door for Ricky Rudd's first road-course win since 1990.

4. Denny Hamlin, Bristol Motor Speedway (2008). Hamlin held the lead with just two laps to go. But then on the final restart, a problem with his fuel pick-up pushed him to a sixth-place finish.

3. Fireball Roberts, Daytona 500 (1959–1961). Often called the best driver to never win a championship, Roberts was no stranger to misfortune. The superstitious driver (who wouldn't even let a girl kiss him before a race because he thought it would bring him bad luck) thought he was jinxed when he lost the first three Daytona 500s in 1959, 1960, and 1961. Then, he broke the spell by winning the Great American Race on his fourth try in 1962.

2. Roush Jinx at Indianapolis Motor Speedway (ongoing). Is it bad luck that no Roush drivers have won at the Brickyard?

1. Dale Earnhardt Sr. in the Daytona 500 (until 1998). It took Dale Earnhardt Sr. 20 tries to win the Daytona 500, and bad luck played a large part in the Intimidator having to wait that long. On five occasions, he was within reach of victory when disaster struck. He ran out of gas (1986), cut a tire on the final lap (1990), hit a seagull and crashed soon after (1991), got passed by Dale Jarrett with just one lap to go (1993), and wrecked while battling for the lead with just 11 laps to go (1997).

One of NASCAR's top all-around drivers, Greg Biffle, has won at least 16 races in three different series—the NASCAR Sprint Cup, the NASCAR Nationwide, and the NASCAR Camping World Truck Series. As a dog lover and cofounder (along with his wife, Nicole) of the Greg Biffle Foundation for Animals, Biffle is also well-qualified to name NASCAR'S "big dogs"—the most influential people in stock car racing. Here are Biffle's picks for the sport's top dogs.

11. Richard Childress. Built a legacy of winners beginning with the legendary No. 3.

10. Rick Hendrick. Runs an absolutely top-notch team.

9. Jack Roush. Consistently competitive team owner.

8. Bruton Smith, chairman, Speedway Motorsports, Inc. Along with his son Marcus Smith, he owns and operates a major track ownership group whose holdings include Bristol Motor Speedway, Charlotte Motor Speedway, and Texas Motor Speedway among other tracks.

7. George Bodenheimer, president of ESPN and ABC Sports, cochairman of Disney Media Networks. Race fans count on ESPN's NASCAR coverage.

6. Dan Hesse, Sprint chairman and CEO. Oversees the sponsorship that keeps the NASCAR Sprint Cup Series running.

5. David Hill, FOX Sports chairman and chief executive. Along with FOX Sports President Ed Goren, Hill has redefined the way racing is covered on TV.

4. John Darby, NASCAR Sprint Cup Series director. He's been referred to as NASCAR's top cop.

3. Robin Pemberton, NASCAR vice president of competition. Runs the competition side of NASCAR.

2. Mike Helton, NASCAR president. His leadership is vital to the sport.

1. The France family. The Alpha Dog spot is shared by NASCAR Chairman of the Board and CEO, Brian France; Vice Chairman, Executive Vice President/Assistant Secretary, Jim France; Vice Chairwoman, Executive Vice President/Assistant Treasurers Lesa Kennedy; and Betty Jane France, Executive Vice President/Assistant Treasurer

What's the first thing most NASCAR drivers do when they win a little prize money? Buy a car. Here are the vehicles that top these drivers' wish lists.

19. Kenny Wallace: Toyota Scion. That's what Kenny says he wants, even though he says his wife thinks it's ugly and won't let him have one. He's been driving a pickup truck for years. The reason? "What if I had to haul something and didn't have a pickup? Then I'd have to borrow one." Regardless, Kenny wants to finally own a car and the inexpensive, gas-efficient Scion is his first choice.

18. Tony Stewart: Army tank. What? He doesn't have one of these already?

17. Joe Nemechek: Hummer. He may not have looked at gas prices lately.

16. Kevin Harvick: Porsche Carrera GT. Sweet, but his wife would kill him for buying such an expensive car.

15. Kurt Busch: his dad's original 1932 Ford. It took Kurt's dad seven years to build this three-window coupe when the Busch brothers were growing up. He sold it so Kurt could go to college and Kurt wants to find it and buy it back for him.

14. Todd Bodine: GTP-type race car. Manufacturer to remain nameless.

13. Martin Truex Jr.: 1969 Camaro. What's not to like?

12. Hermie Sadler: mid-1970s Corvette. Inspired by the movie *Corvette Summer*.

11. Greg Biffle: Ford GT-40. Absolutely awesome, according to the Biff.

10. Mike Skinner: Lexus LFA. Pricey, according to Skinner, it's like a Formula One car you can drive on the street. Plan B is a 1969 Supersport Chevelle.

9. Broadcaster Barney Hall: his old '47 Dodge. He dreams about his old two-door coupe every day.

8. Ron Hornaday: ZO6 Corvette. But really, he likes to buy things and restore them himself.

7. Kyle Petty: an old-school bobber/chopper with a Victory motorcycle engine on it. Sounds like KP has given this some thought.

6. Matt Kenseth: Porsche Carrera GT. Inspired by Rick Hendrick.

5. Robby Gordon: his own off-road truck. Let's just say it's modified.

4. Boris Said: Robby Gordon's off-road truck. Off-road envy.

3. Jon Wood: limo. No telling what the Wood Brothers might do to one of those.

2. Michael Waltrip: Corvette. One of those Z06s.

1. Brian Vickers: Corvette. He wants to let his dad drive it.

They say a race car driver is a race car driver, no matter what his vehicle of choice might be. But some drivers have proven their versatility in NASCAR by competing and winning across every one of the three top series.

Here are the 22 drivers who have scored a win in all three NASCAR series—with their number of wins in each series (listed in order of NASCAR Sprint Cup, NASCAR Nationwide, and NASCAR Camping World Truck Series) followed by their total number of wins as of September 6, 2011.

22. David Reutimann. 2, 1, 1 (total: 4).

21. Steve Park. 2, 3, 1 (total: 6).

20. Ricky Craven. 2, 4, 1 (total: 7).

19. Ken Schrader. 4, 2, 1 (total: 7).

18. Elliott Sadler. 3, 5, 1 (total: 9).

17. Clint Bowyer. 4, 8, 3 (total: 15).

16. Jamie McMurray. 6, 8, 1 (total: 15).

15. Jimmy Spencer. 2, 12, 1 (total: 15).

14. Bobby Hamilton. 4, 1, 10 (total: 15).

13. Michael Waltrip. 4, 11, 1 (total: 16).

12. Johnny Benson. 1, 3, 14 (total: 18).

11. Kasey Kahne. 11, 7, 3 (total: 21).

10. Ryan Newman. 15, 7, 1 (total: 23).

9. Kurt Busch. 23, 3, 4 (total: 30).

8. Bobby Labonte. 21, 10, 1 (total: 32).

7. Terry Labonte. 22, 11, 1 (total: 34).

6. Tony Stewart. 39, 10, 2 (total: 51).

5. Greg Biffle. 16, 20, 16 (total: 52).

4. Carl Edwards. 19, 35, 6 (total: 60).

3. Kevin Harvick. 17, 37, 12 (total: 66).

2. Mark Martin. 40, 49, 7 (total: 96).

1. Kyle Busch. 23, 50, 29 (total: 102).

Best All-Around Drivers

Only three drivers have won in all three series in the same year. One driver has done it once, one driver has done it twice, and one overachiever has done it an incredible seven times. Here are the years, the drivers, their wins by series (NASCAR Sprint Cup, Nationwide, and Camping World Truck Series), and the total wins for these well-rounded guys.

10. Terry Labonte (1995). 3, 1, 1 (total: 5).

9. Kevin Harvick (2003). 1, 3, 1 (total: 5).

8. Kyle Busch (2005). 2, 1, 3 (total: 6).

7. Kyle Busch (2006). 1, 1, 1 (total: 3).

6. Kyle Busch (2007). 1, 4, 2 (total: 6).

5. Kyle Busch (2008). 8, 10, 3 (total: 21).

4. Kyle Busch (2009). 4, 9, 7 (total: 20).

3. Kevin Harvick (2010). 3, 3, 3 (total: 9).

2. Kyle Busch (2010). 3, 13, 8 (total: 24).

1. Kyle Busch (2011). 4, 8, 6 (total: 18, as of October 2, 2011).

Most Coors Light Pole Awards in a Single Season

The fastest driver during qualifying wins the Coors Light Pole Award and starts the race at the front of the pack. That's a very good place to be, but just because a driver starts in first, doesn't mean he will finish in first. A good example is Ryan Newman, who has 49 career Coors Light Pole Awards through September 25, 2011, to his credit. But in those races that he has started first, Newman has won only three times. Geoffrey Bodine, with 37 career Coors Light Pole Awards, won from the front position only four times. Ricky Rudd? Only one victory from 29 career poles. Alan Kulwicki? Just one win from 24.

Switching to a more positive perspective on the pole, some drivers have a knack for taking the Coors Light Pole Award at certain race tracks. Ryan Newman won six consecutive Coors Light Pole Awards at Atlanta Motor Speedway. For David Pearson, Charlotte Motor Speedway was his sweet spot; he won 11 straight Coors Light Pole Awards there.

Here are the drivers who claimed the most Coors Light Pole Awards in a single season.

8. Fonty Flock (1951), 13.

7. Bobby Isaac (1970), 13.

6. David Pearson (1969), 14.

5. Cale Yarborough (1980), 14.

4. Richard Petty (1966), 15.

3. Tim Flock (1955), 18.

2. Richard Petty (1967), 18.

1. Bobby Isaac (1969), 19.

Most All-Time Wins from the Coors Light Pole Award Position

Pretty self-explanatory, except the asterisk, which means the total includes at least one Coors Light Pole Award in a race where no qualifying was held.

16. Fonty Flock, 10.

15. Jimmie Johnson, 10.*

14. Fred Lorenzen, 11.

13. Ned Jarrett, 11.

12. Junior Johnson, 12.*

11. Buck Baker, 13.

10. Cale Yarborough, 16.*

9. Tim Flock, 17.

8. Bill Elliott, 17.*

7. Herb Thomas, 19.

6. Jeff Gordon, 19.

5. Bobby Allison, 20.

4. Bobby Isaac, 21.*

3. Darrell Waltrip, 24.

2. David Pearson, 37.

1. Richard Petty, 61.

Shady Characters

Whether it's sunny outside or pouring down rain, count on NASCAR drivers to be wearing their sunglasses. Some drivers have become so identified with their shades that they are hardly recognizable without them.

Maybe it's a generational thing. Darrell Waltrip recently complimented Jamie McMurray for showing up for a TV interview *not* wearing sunglasses. This has become a rarity. Here are our picks for the shadiest characters in stock car racing.

10. Tony Stewart. The sometimes-polarizing driver swears by his polarized pair.

9. (tie) Carl Edwards, Mark Martin, and Denny Hamlin. Wiley X eyewear all around.

8. Elliott Sadler. His white glasses are gaudy, but look closely—there's an Autism Speaks logo on the frame, so these specs serve a good cause.

7. Kyle Busch. Bloggers pick on Busch for his oversized shades. If he doesn't like it, he needs to stop wearing shades the size of his head.

6. (tie) Dale Earnhardt Jr. and Martin Truex Jr. The Juniors choose Spy glasses. All the kids are wearing them.

5. Jeff Gordon. Is that the four-time champ behind those Foster Grants?

4. Juan Pablo Montoya. The first NASCAR driver to don a pair of white Oakleys.

3. Kasey Kahne. When he was named one of *People Magazine*'s Top 50 Bachelors, his Oakleys became a must.

2. The Intimidator. Dale Earnhardt became famous for his patented wraparounds.

1. The King. Richard Petty started the trend. He never goes anywhere without his trademark shades.

Most Consecutive Starts

Sometimes the hardest part of anything is getting started. In NASCAR, all great finishes begin at the start/finish line. Showing up and competing consistently is a huge accomplishment. So here's a nod to the drivers who have scored the most consecutive NASCAR Sprint Cup Series starts. (Note: a single asterisk indicates an active driver and active streak, with the streak total as of August 27, 2011; a double asterisk indicates an active driver whose listed streak has been broken.)

10. Richard Petty, 513.

9. Jeff Burton, 544.*

8. Ken Schrader, 579.**

7. Mark Martin, 621.**

6. Bobby Labonte, 640.*

5. Jeff Gordon, 641.*

4. Dale Earnhardt Sr, 648.

3. Terry Labonte, 655.**

2. Rusty Wallace, 697.

1. Ricky Rudd, 788.

And here's a nod to the drivers who have started the most (non-consecutive) NASCAR Sprint Cup Series races in their careers as of October 2, 2011, with their number of career wins also listed. (Note: an asterisk indicates a driver who is still active, as of the 2011 season.)

25. Geoffrey Bodine, 572 starts (18 wins).*

24. David Pearson, 574 starts (105 wins).

23. Joe Nemecheck, 580 starts (4 wins).*

22. James Hylton, 602 starts (2 wins).

21. Jeff Burton, 607 starts (20 wins).*

20. Buck Baker, 636 starts (46 wins).

19. Jeff Gordon, 646 starts (85 wins).*

18. Bobby Labonte, 647 starts (21 wins).*

17. J.D. McDuffie, 653 starts (0 wins).

16. Dale Jarrett, 668 starts (32 wins).

15. Dale Earnhardt Sr, 676 starts (76 wins).

14. Buddy Baker, 699 starts (19 wins).

13. Rusty Wallace, 706 starts (55 wins).

12. Bobby Allison, 718 starts (84 wins).

11. Ken Schrader, 739 starts (4 wins).*

10. Sterling Marlin, 748 starts (10 wins).

9. Michael Waltrip, 765 starts (four wins).*

8. Darrell Waltrip, 809 starts (84 wins).

7. Mark Martin, 823 starts (40 wins).*

6. Bill Elliott, 826 starts (44 wins).*

5. Kyle Petty, 829 starts (eight wins).

4. Terry Labonte, 876 starts (22 wins).*

3. Dave Marcis, 883 starts (five wins).

2. Ricky Rudd, 906 starts (23 wins).

1. Richard Petty, 1,185 starts (200 wins).

Every NASCAR fan knows that Jimmie Johnson has won five championships, that Jimmy Spencer drove aggressively, and that Darrell Waltrip is never shy when it comes to public speaking. But there are some things fans may not know. For instance, did you know that . . .

18. Mike Skinner. Is a wine connoisseur with an incredibly impressive wine cellar.

17. Brian Vickers. Skipped his high school prom in Thomasville, North Carolina, to go racing.

16. Dale Jarrett. Is a great golfer who once considered going pro.

15. Kurt Busch. Is really good at archery. Or so he says.

14. Ryan Newman. Has an engineering degree from Purdue University.

13. David Reutimann. Drives the No. 00 car because he and his father, who also drove the No. 00, spent all their money on racing when they were regulars at dirt tracks.

12. Carl Edwards. Was a pole-vaulter in high school.

11. Chad Little. Has a law degree from Gonzaga University.

10. Geoffrey Bodine. Helped design the four-man bobsled that won a gold medal for the U.S. at the 2010 Winter Olympics in Vancouver.

9. Derrike Cope. Was a standout high school and college baseball player who turned down offers from the Baltimore Orioles and Chicago Cubs before going into racing.

8. Kenny Wallace. Routinely gets his eyebrows waxed.

7. Cale Yarborough. Has been bitten by a rattlesnake, hit by lightning, and wrestled an alligator. Not all on the same day.

6. Kyle Petty. Was once an aspiring country singer who shared an apartment with country star Marty Stuart.

5. Elliott Sadler. Played college basketball (briefly) for Hall of Fame Coach Lefty Driesell at James Madison University in Virginia.

4. Tony Stewart. Bought the Columbus, Indiana, home he grew up in and still lives there.

3. Richard Petty. Almost broke off a lucrative sponsorship deal with STP during negotiations because STP wanted the car to be totally red and Petty wanted it to be all Petty blue. Obviously, they compromised.

2. Junior Johnson. Was given a presidential pardon by Ronald Reagan.

1. Mike Harmon. Granted a late fan's last wish when he taped an urn (containing the fan's ashes) to the fire extinguisher of his car during a NASCAR Nationwide Series practice and gave him a ride around the track at the Las Vegas Motor Speedway.

Even though fans think NASCAR drivers are living a dream (and most drivers would agree with that), a driver can still dream about doing other things as well. And many drivers dream about playing in a band. Some guys, such as country star and part-time NASCAR driver Marty Robbins, actually display real talent. Others are best relegated to singing in the shower. Here's the dream band of NASCAR drivers we would put together, if we could.

9. Big Bill France: ukulele. The image of the big man playing the tiny instrument is priceless.

8. Marty Robbins: lead guitar and vocals. Rumor had it that he sang "El Paso" while driving around the track.

7. Kyle Petty: guitar, backup vocals. Kyle Petty once thought he might be bound for stardom in the world of country music.

6. Tony Stewart: trombone. Tony played the instrument in high school. If our band decides we don't need a horn, he can play bass guitar, which he's been learning to play for awhile now.

5. Bobby Allison, Darrell Waltrip, Buddy Baker, David Pearson, Richard Petty, and Cale Yarborough: backup vocals. In the 1970s, this all-star group recorded an album, *NASCAR Goes Country*. They seriously did. Baker's performance of "Butterbeans" put him in the running for lead singer, but Robbins won out. Since the group is already proficient in a NASCAR-specific rendition of "99 Bottles of Beer," the dream band may consider including this on our set list.

4. Michael Waltrip: piano. Have you seen the NAPA commercial? Mikey's Jerry Lee Lewis impression leaves no doubt that this guy can tickle the ivories.

3. Dale Earnhardt Jr.: backup vocals. He's a seasoned pro after performing "Where I'm From" with country star Kenny Chesney at the Dale Earnhardt Tribute Concert in 2003.

2. John Roberts and Rutledge Wood (SPEED Channel): drums. Both of us play. All the better to drown out our singing.

1. Carl Edwards: guitar. Carl played drums in high school marching band. But since we've already seated a drum section, Carl can play guitar.

Plan B

Most NASCAR drivers dreamed of driving a race car for a living from the time they were old enough to grab onto a steering wheel. But what if the driving thing hadn't worked out? Here are the careers that several drivers said they might have pursued.

12. Dale Earnhardt Jr. Mechanic.

11. Jeff Gordon. Real estate agent.

10. Carl Edwards. Pilot in the air force or navy.

9. Kurt Busch. Photographer.

8. Kyle Busch. His mom wanted him to be a dentist.

7. Jimmie Johnson. Firefighter.

6. Mark Martin. Nothing.

5. Ryan Newman. Engineer.

4. Chad Little. Lawyer.

3. Kyle Petty. Country music singer.

2. Michael Waltrip. Stand-up comedian.

1. Tony Stewart. Didn't have an answer. To Smoke, there is only one job.

Plan 2-B

Here are the alternate careers that we think several drivers could have also excelled in.

7. Curtis Turner. Stunt pilot.

6. Richard Petty. United Nations ambassador or U.S. president.

5. Junior Johnson. College football coach.

4. Tim Flock. Zookeeper.

3. Danica Patrick. Astronaut.

2. Trevor Bayne. Competitive wakeboarder.

1. Darrell Waltrip. Talk-show host.

It's unusual for a NASCAR driver to have a one-track mind. Because they are athletes and competitors, most drivers follow other sports and have favorite players and teams. Here are some driver favorites.

12. Denny Hamlin. Charlotte Bobcats season ticket holder. Sponsored by Nike's Air Jordan brand.

11. Brian Vickers. Charlotte Bobcats, Carolina Panthers, New York Giants, and New York Yankees.

10. Carl Edwards. Boston Red Sox and Albert Pujols of the St. Louis Cardinals.

9. Aric Almirola. Golf (Tiger Woods) and baseball (although he'd rather play it than watch it). Favorite baseball players growing up were Barry Larkin and Cal Ripken Jr.

8. Kurt Busch. Chicago Cubs, Ryne Sandberg.

7. Kyle Busch. Denver Broncos, John Elway.

6. Matt Kenseth. Green Bay Packers.

5. Jeff Gordon. San Francisco 49ers, Joe Montana.

4. Dale Earnhardt Jr. Washington Redskins.

3. Jimmie Johnson. USA in the Olympics.

2. Tony Stewart. Indianapolis Colts, Peyton Manning.

1. Kyle Petty. Loves watching the Golf Channel.

Some drivers seem to have success the minute they show up at the track. Or do they? In the formative years of the sport, overnight success stories were not unusual. Drivers would show up out of nowhere and win, but more often than not, they would hardly be heard from again.

In the modern era (post-1972), it actually takes some time for most drivers to start racking up wins. Drivers who win right away are rarities.

Here are some of the drivers who won a NASCAR Sprint Cup Series race early in their careers, along with the career start they won it in.

Fifth Career Start

5. Lee Petty. October 2, 1949, Heidelberg Raceway, Pittsburgh, Pennsylvania.

4. Marshall Teague. February 11, 1951, Daytona Beach & Road Course, Daytona Beach, Florida.

3. Tommy Thompson. August 12, 1951, Michigan State Fairgrounds, Detroit, Michigan.

2. Danny Weinberg. October 28, 1951, Marchbanks Speedway, Hanford, California.

1. Mark Donohue. January 21, 1973. Riverside International Raceway, Riverside, California.

Fourth Career Start

2. Curtis Turner. September 11, 1949, Langhorne Speedway, Langhorne, Pennsylvania.

1. Jimmy Florian. June 25, 1950, Dayton Speedway, Dayton, Ohio.

Third Career Start

7. Bob Flock. August 7, 1949, Occoneechee Speedway, Hillsboro, North Carolina.

6. Fireball Roberts. August 13, 1950, Occoneechee Speedway, Hillsboro, North Carolina.

5. Johnny Mantz. September 4, 1950, Darlington Raceway, Darlington, South Carolina.

4. Bill Norton. November 11, 1951, Carrell Speedway, Gardena, California.

3. John Soares. May 30, 1954, Carrell Speedway, Gardena, California.

2. Dan Gurney. January 20, 1963, Riverside International Raceway, Riverside, California.

1. Kevin Harvick. March 11, 2001, Atlanta Motor Speedway, Hampton, Georgia.

Second Career Start

6. Red Byron. July 10, 1949, Daytona Beach & Road Course, Daytona Beach, Florida.

5. Norm Nelson. October 16, 1955, Las Vegas Park Speedway, Las Vegas, Nevada.

4. Chuck Stevenson. November 20, 1955, Willow Springs Speedway, Lancaster, California.

3. John Rostek. April 3, 1960, Arizona State Fairgrounds, Phoenix, Arizona.

2. Jamie McMurray. October 13, 2002, Charlotte Motor Speedway, Concord, North Carolina.

1. Trevor Bayne. February 20, 2011, Daytona International Speedway, Daytona Beach, Florida.

First Career Start

6. Jim Roper. June 19, 1949, Charlotte Speedway, Charlotte, North Carolina.

5. Jack White. September 18, 1949, Hamburg Speedway, Hamburg, New York.

4. Harold Kite. February 5, 1950, Daytona Beach & Road Course, Daytona Beach, Florida.

3. Leon Sales. September 24, 1950, North Wilkesboro Speedway, North Wilkesboro, North Carolina.

2. Marvin Burke. October 14, 1951, Oakland Stadium, Oakland, California.

1. Johnny Rutherford. February 22, 1963, Daytona International Speedway, Daytona Beach, Florida.

No one questions that NASCAR drivers have the moves on the track. But off the track, sometimes drivers get, well, off track. Here are some of the less-than-brilliant moves we've seen from them over the years.

7. Jack Sprague. When NASCAR Camping World Truck Series driver Jack Sprague fell off a ladder while cleaning leaves out of his gutters, he gave fellow drivers a ready-made excuse to skip out on household chores.

6. Denny Hamlin. Following testing at Charlotte Motor Speedway in 2006, Denny Hamlin gashed his hand on a protruding piece of metal while partaking in a foot race around his hauler. (Despite the injury, Denny won the NASCAR Nationwide Series race at Darlington the following week.)

5. Carl Edwards. As it was pointed out many times following this incident, here's a guy who does backflips on asphalt and concrete, and he breaks his foot playing Ultimate Frisbee. Second prize goes to "Cousin Carl" for slicing his finger open while grating cheese at an Asphalt Chef competition at Texas Motor Speedway.

4. Jimmie Johnson. Broke his hand falling off a golf cart.

3. Kyle Petty. Blowing off steam after losing a race, Kyle Petty punched the side of a trailer and hurt his hand. When Jimmie Johnson's PR rep asked him what happened, Petty deadpanned, "I fell off a golf cart."

2. Dale Earnhardt Jr. After winning the fall race at Talladega in 2004, Dale Jr. was asked by a reporter what it meant to win at a track his father had so utterly dominated. Junior's reply? "It don't mean sh*t." The comment cost him $10,000 and 25 championship points.

1. Kyle Busch. Just prior to the 2011 Coca-Cola 600, Busch was ticketed for doing 128 mph in a yellow Lexus LFA on a two-lane, 45 mph road in Troutman, North Carolina. Busch told the officer he was testing out the new car and got carried away.

Imagine this: you're moving at over 180 mph, there are two people telling you what to do in your ear, it's over 100 degrees in your office, and a split-second decision can cost you millions. No pressure. Just the life of a NASCAR driver.

With all that in mind, it's a miracle that more drivers don't make huge mistakes on the race track. Here are just a few of the blunders that stand out.

14. Where's Victory Lane? When he won the 2011 Daytona 500, Trevor Bayne took a slight wrong turn and passed the entrance to Victory Lane. He radioed his crew for directions and found it soon enough, though.

13. Tire Stall. During a late 1990s race at Bristol, Jeff Gordon was leading when he slammed into a tire in Steve Park's pit stall as he was returning to the track following a pit stop during a caution. He fell from first place to 17th place.

12. Outburst. Newcomer Jerry Nadeau had never before led a lap in a NASCAR Sprint Cup Series race when he started in the front row with Coors Light Pole Award winner Jeff Gordon at Infineon Raceway in 1998. Just after the green flag dropped, Nadeau floored it and made a move on Gordon to take the lead for a millisecond before careening off the road course into the dirt. He recovered and got back on track, but never regained his favorable position.

11. In This Corner. During the Texas race in 2010, Jeff Burton drilled Jeff Gordon into the wall under caution. The goof infuriated Gordon, who hopped out of the car to confront Burton, who joined him in putting on a mixed martial arts exhibition.

10. One-Finger Salute. At the same Texas race, Kyle Busch was penalized for speeding on pit road. He was then penalized another two laps for unsportsmanlike conduct when he was caught on live TV flipping the bird to NASCAR officials.

9. A Moment Too Soon. Toward the end of Richard Petty's famous 200th win at Daytona in 1984, Cale Yarborough thought the race was over and pulled into pit road one lap early.

8. Stuck. Matt Kenseth lists his most embarrassing on-track moment as the time he was trying to get on pit road in Dover and ended up on top of the tires like a monster truck. Unfortunately for Kenseth, it's often featured on a highlight reel played on the big screen at Dover.

7. Running on Fumes. Dale Jarrett was leading the 1998 Brickyard at the halfway point when he ran out of gas and was forced to pit. He got back on the lead lap, but never regained the lead after the embarrassing fuel miscalculation. He made up for it by winning the same race the following year.

6. Jeff Gordon's Spin. After starting from the pole, and leading for a race-high 51 laps at Watkins Glen in 2007, Jeff Gordon was in sight of his 10th road-course victory. Then with just two laps to go, Gordon inexplicably spun out while heading into the first turn. He'd lost the lead—and the race—all by himself.

5. Mark Martin's Miscount. On Lap 249 of the 250-lap NASCAR Nationwide Series Race in Bristol in 1994, leader Mark Martin pulled into pit road en route to Victory Lane. The only problem was, the race still had a lap to go. Martin had miscounted and finished 11th as a result of his mathematical mistake.

4. Bumper Cars. With just three laps remaining in the 2002 Daytona 500, Sterling Marlin crunched his right fender in a collision with Jeff Gordon. A multicar accident followed and race officials threw the red flag. Then, as a stunned TV audience watched, Marlin, still on the track, hopped out of his car and attempted to shove his fender back into place.

Following the infraction, Marlin was sent to the back of the lead-lap cars for the restart. "I saw Earnhardt do it at Richmond one time in 1986," Marlin said. "He got out and cleaned his windshield, so I thought it was OK."

3. Tiny Lund's Run-In. During an accident at the Nashville 400 in the 1960s, Cale Yarborough dodged the wrecked cars in front of him, but not driver Tiny Lund, who had climbed from his car and was running across the track. According to Yarborough, Lund ran right into his door and bent the whole door in. Lund was unhurt.

2. Marcos Ambrose Engine Shut Down. At the 2010 Infineon race, Ambrose made one of the biggest blunders in recent NASCAR history when he stalled his car under caution while leading late in the race. Ambrose was cutting his engine off to save fuel, but when it stalled, he had to give up his position on the track and, ultimately, lost the race to Jimmie Johnson.

1. Buddy Baker Gets the Ride of His Life. At a 1967 race in Maryville, Tennessee, Baker cut a tire and his car went headfirst into the wall. Two emergency workers attempted to pull an injured Baker from the car while he was still strapped in. Then the workers loaded Baker onto a stretcher and into the back of an ambulance, but they forgot to lock down the wheels of the stretcher. They also forgot to lock the ambulance's back door.

As the ambulance started up the high bank to leave the track, the doors flew open and Baker, strapped to the stretcher, rolled out onto the track, where cars, although under caution, were still flying by. The cars dodged the stretcher as it rolled across and then off the track. It finally stopped in the grassy area next to the pavement and flipped Baker face-first into the mud.

Although not technically Baker's blunder, this on-track goof is a classic.

NASCAR has more than its fair share of rags-to-riches stories. Many of the old-timers had to scrape together money just to enter a race, then win enough money in the race to make it to the next track. Most of today's up-and-coming drivers may not have had to choose between eating and buying new tires very often, but there are plenty of examples of young drivers sleeping in their cars or risking everything to claw their way to the top of the racing world. It takes time to make it to NASCAR's top tier. Or, as Dale Jarrett always said, it took him 12 years to become an overnight sensation. Here are some favorite Cinderella stories.

14. (tie) Greg Biffle and Clint Bowyer. Both welded in their fathers' shops while waiting to get the call to go big-time racing.

13. Matt Kenseth. Long before he was a NASCAR Sprint Cup Series champion, a very young Matt Kenseth helped his dad deliver furniture to put spending money in his pocket.

12. Carl Edwards. When he was in high school, Edwards printed up business cards that read, "If you're looking for a driver, you're looking for me." He handed them out by the dozens, hoping for his big break. When he started competing at dirt tracks, he borrowed money from his mother (which he has since paid back) and worked odd jobs, including substitute teaching, to support his racing habit. He also slept in his car as he traveled from dirt track to dirt track.

11. Alan Kulwicki. He hit the NASCAR circuit with a borrowed pickup truck, his race car, and no sponsor.

10. Ned Jarrett. As a young, up-and-coming driver, Jarrett once wrote a $2,000 check for a car on a Friday afternoon after the banks had closed. Over the weekend, he won two races and deposited the prize money in the bank on Monday morning, just in time to cover the check.

9. Mark Martin. After his first year as a NASCAR competitor, Mark Martin auctioned off his shop equipment to pay his bills. He had to start from scratch the following year.

8. Bobby Allison. The 2011 NASCAR Hall of Fame Inductee started out sweeping the floors in the garage.

7. Tony Stewart. He once borrowed the entry fee for a race from his girlfriend. He often slept on people's couches when he went on the road and back home in Indiana, he worked at Dairy Queen.

6. Steve Park. He worked long nights at his auto repair business and once completely ran out of money after producing a $15,000 promotional video in an attempt to recruit sponsors.

5. Kenny Wallace. He cleaned septic tanks while his dad and brother earned their money at the race track

4. Bobby Labonte. He worked as a janitor pushing a broom and emptying trash cans.

3. Ernie Irvan. Before he made his NASCAR Sprint Cup Series debut in 1987, Irvan worked as a welder (repairing seats) at Charlotte Motor Speedway. He also loaded and unloaded equipment for NASCAR Sprint Cup driver Ken Schrader.

2. Bobby Isaac. The son of a mill worker and sibling to eight brothers and sisters, Isaac didn't own a pair of shoes until he was 13 years old. He quit school in the sixth grade, racked balls in a pool hall and hitchhiked around town. Finally, at age 24, he set his sights on racing and became a NASCAR Sprint Cup champion.

1. Dale Earnhardt Sr. The future Intimidator dropped out of the eighth grade to become a race car driver. During his early days, Earnhardt would borrow money on Fridays to buy tires for the Saturday race, knowing that if he didn't win enough money, he couldn't pay back the money he borrowed.

Every athlete knows about slumps. Whether you're a pitcher, a quarterback, or a NASCAR Sprint Cup Series driver, when you get in one, it's often tough to get out. Just ask Dale Earnhardt Jr., who passed the 100-race winless mark in June 2011, or Ken Schrader, the active driver with the longest unbroken winless streak (523, as of June 2011).

The good news for the drivers on this list is that they did in fact snap their respective streaks and score another win or wins. Here is our list of the unlucky 13 drivers who endured lengthy slumps that thankfully came to an end.

13. Ryan Newman. People may not have noticed, but Ryan Newman set the all-time record for going winless in 35 straight races that he started from the pole. I'm sure he appreciates the shout-out.

12. Jeff Gordon. Plenty of drivers have lost dozens of races in a row. But when you're Jeff Gordon, people notice. He broke his 60-race winless streak at Phoenix in 2011.

11. Matt Kenseth. By dominating and winning the 2011 race at Texas, Matt Kenseth returned to Victory Lane after 76 consecutive misses.

10. Carl Edwards. Broke a 70-race losing run at Phoenix in 2010.

9. Mark Martin. As a driver who's been around for awhile, Martin knows patience pays. He's snapped winless streaks of 109 (at Phoenix in 2009) and 72 (at Dover in 2004).

8. Jeremy Mayfield. A win at Richmond in September 2004 broke Mayfield's winless run going back to 2000. The cliff-hanger win also memorably grabbed him a spot in that year's Chase for the NASCAR Sprint Cup.

7. Kevin Harvick. Adapted and overcame, following a 115-race slump.

6. Dale Jarrett. The 1999 NASCAR Sprint Cup champ once endured a 128-race winless streak.

5. Sterling Marlin. No one expected Sterling Marlin, who won his first two NASCAR Sprint Cup races in the Daytona 500, to ride his way into a five-season slump. But he did. He broke it in a big way by winning at Michigan International Speedway in 2001 for his seventh NASCAR Sprint Cup victory and the first win for Dodge in 24 years.

4. Jeff Burton. A six-season, 185-race slump finally ended for Burton at Dover in 2006.

3. Fireball Roberts. In an era where drivers ran many more races than they do today, it took Fireball Roberts six years to finally work his way out of a slump that finally ended in 1956.

2. Wood Brothers Racing. When their driver Trevor Bayne took the checkered flag at the Daytona 500 in 2011, the legendary Wood Brothers broke a decade-long winless streak.

1. Michael Waltrip. The longest winless streak in the modern era goes to Michael Waltrip, who suffered through 462 losses before scoring a win in 2001. And Mikey made it a big one, breaking out of his slump at the Daytona 500.

Race fans not planning to apply for a job on a pit crew don't necessarily have to know that a carburetor is mounted on top of the intake manifold or that viscosity decreases as oil gets hotter. You don't even really have to know what viscosity is. But certain words are thrown around regularly enough that fans will want to know what the heck they mean. Here are the terms that every race fan should know.

17. Apron. Not the thing your mom wears in the kitchen. At a race, the apron is the paved part of the track that separates the racing surface from the infield.

16. Banking. Has nothing to do with visiting the ATM before purchasing an all-inclusive race weekend package. In NASCAR, banking refers to the slope of a race track—specifically at a curve or a turn—from the apron to the outside wall.

15. Checkered. Has nothing to do with a shady past. Refers to the black-and-white flag waved at the end of the race to signify a win.

14. Chute. Rather than a shaft to throw your laundry into or a necessary piece of skydiving equipment, at the race track, "chute" means the track straightaway.

13. Dirty Air. In this case, "dirty" refers not to pollution but rather turbulent air caused by fast moving cars that could cause one of the cars to lose control.

12. Drafting. Has nothing to do with being called into the armed services. When you see two or more cars running nose-to-tail, that's drafting. The first car cuts the air for the car or cars right behind it, while those cars return a smoother airflow over the first car, creating a vacuum effect. Bottom line: everyone goes faster.

11. Groove. This is a term for the best route around the race track. Has nothing to do with rhythm.

10. Loose. In NASCAR, "loose" describes when the rear end of a car starts to lose its grip and slide, or fishtail, especially when the car takes fast corners.

9. Marbles. In NASCAR, these are rubber (built up pieces left on the track), not glass.

8. Pit Road. The section of pavement alongside the track where drivers go to get their tires changed and have their crews make minor (and hopefully, very speedy) repairs. It's uncool to call this place "pit row." NASCAR aficionados know that there is no such thing.

7. Pole (Coors Light Pole Award). Awarded to the driver who was fastest during qualifying, the pole is the best place (the inside position on the first row) to start the race.

6. Restrictor Plate. Not the diet special featured at your local diner. In NASCAR, this is a very important four-holed thin metal plate that restricts airflow from the carburetor to the engine in order to reduce speeds on cars running on the tracks at Daytona and Talladega.

5. Slick. It seems like stating the obvious to define "slick" as the condition in which a race car has difficulty adhering to the track surface. But be advised, a track can be slick even when there is no sign of oil or water on the surface.

4. Splash 'n' Go. At NASCAR tracks, this refers to a pit stop during which a driver takes on just a splash of fuel.

3. Spoiler. In the regular world, this refers to a guy who tells you the ending of a movie before you've had a chance to see it. In NASCAR, we're talking about a metal blade attached to the rear deck lid of the car to help provide downforce and traction.

2. Tight. Does not reference the guy who never picks up the check for dinner. When a driver describes his car as "tight," he's telling the crew chief that the front wheels lose traction before the rear wheels and it's tough to steer through the turns.

1. Wedge. Not the iceberg lettuce salad with blue cheese or the thing your big brother used to give you. In NASCAR, this describes the cross weight adjustment on a race car.

Twitter

Not long ago, most people in NASCAR thought that a tweet was the sound made by the seagull that Michael Waltrip hit during Daytona qualifying. But today, everybody knows about social media—blogging, Facebook, and Twitter—and no one denies that it is a powerful force.

Twitter is especially popular. Of the 190 million tweets sent daily, a big chunk of them are from the world of NASCAR. Team owners and drivers, such as Juan Pablo Montoya, who currently has the most followers, use Twitter to make announcements or to get people talking or even to get into their competitors' heads.

Kenny Wallace, who has 50,000 followers, used Facebook and Twitter to successfully pursue sponsorship for the 2009 NASCAR Nationwide Series race in Montreal. (He signed up 7,000 sponsors for his fan car.) Another time, Kenny sent a tweet from a Porta-Potty in Martinsville and let the fans know that he was indeed "talking" to them from the toilet. According to Kenny, fans related, responded, and kept the thread going for three days—his largest response to a tweet to date.

Kyle Petty is an active Twitter user. When he sends out a provocative tweet and fans get riled up, what does he do? He sends it out again (re-tweets).

Drivers have learned they need to watch what they say on Twitter. Denny Hamlin was fined in 2010 for comments he made about caution flags following a NASCAR Nationwide race at Chicagoland Speedway.

Jamie McMurray says, "Whenever I tweet, it has to be something I would be OK with my mom reading."

Fans and media people need to beware of impostors (there are tons of fake Dale Jr.'s) or misinformation on tweets. In April 2010, Texas Motor Speedway fooled several news outlets via a fake story about a local DJ changing his name to Texasmotorspeedway.com for $100,000.

Keeping all that in mind, here are some memorable recent series of tweets. (Note: remember to send yours to twitter@racedayonspeed).

9. Exchange between Jimmie Johnson, Ryan McGee, and Marty Smith.

RyanMcGeeESPN @JimmieJohnson @MartySmithESPN Greatest all-time inventions: 4.Soap 3.Wheel 2.Gold Bond menthol 1.WD40

JimmieJohnson @RyanMcGeeESPN @MartySmithESPN I must say I agree. Toothpaste is ahead of WD40 for me though.

RyanMcGeeESPN @JimmieJohnson @MartySmithESPN Imagine how clean your teeth could be if they put a little WD40 in the toothpaste

JimmieJohnson @RyanMcGeeESPN @MartySmithESPN That's your billion dollar invention! Get on it!

RyanMcGeeESPN @JimmieJohnson @MartySmithESPN Sweet. Get me a meeting with someone at Lowe's!

8. Kevin Harvick tweets.

KevinHarvick Ground hogs are back!! Screw dinner I am going hunting!

KevinHarvick Good news smoke alarm works in bus bad news is I can't get the smoke to clear out . . . candle in the back was a smoker . . .

7. Jimmie Johnson and Brad Keselowski tweets.

KristineC48 (Kristine Curley, P.R. Rep) As @jimmiejohnson was signing his hat a teenager asked JJ: "Going for 6?" JJ: "Nah . . . "

keselowski There are thousands of ways to pay someone back. I won't be mad if or when it happens to me. Sign of weakness.

keselowski C'mon Just watching *Sportscenter* recap of nw race. #trainwreck Announcer actually said, "another case of poor fuel management."

keselowski I get that not every announcer is gonna know everything about every sport. But isn't that why 2 are used for *Sportscenter*? #justsayin

JimmieJohnson: Congrats on last week, I'm not sure I've said anything yet.

keselowski @JimmieJohnson: Thanks bro Congrats on the last 5 years, not sure if I said it ;)

6. Kenny Wallace tweets.

Kenny Wallace Been gone 3 weeks from my wife! . . She looks GOOD "All Tanned up" Whooo Hooo! . . Thank You Jack Roush, We r flying on his Plane:)

Kenny Wallace I use twitter for therapy!. . I like people to hear me also!. . And yes I do seek attention because I have 3rd child Syndrome!

Kenny Wallace I have noticed that I am close to 50 Thousand followers!. . Why do you ALL Follow me?. .I am a Weirdo!

5. Joey Logano tweets.

JLogano The AC broke in our rental and it's real hot out. So me and my old man are going up the highway with the windows down and our shirts off haha

JLogano So I just found someone stole my golf cart last night while I was sleeping. It's been a rough speed weeks but it can only go up from here.

4. John Roberts tweets.

Speedtv_JR Two new wines from Childress Vineyards Busch Blush and Upper Cut Cuvee

Speedtv_JR OK Why did Kevorkian swab alcohol on the arm of the dude he was hooking up to the suicide machine? Think he worried about infection?

Speedtv_JR Why does Fred Flintstone order the same ribs at the end of every show when he knows they will tip his car over?

Speedtv_JR Yes! I found it. A tee shirt older than Trevor Bayne I knew I had one

Speedtv_JR Finally Congress has done something good. They voted to turn down the volume on commercials!

3. Miscellaneous tweets.

Tbayne21 (Trevor Bayne) Hangin out on the side of I-77 waitin on @justinjj21 to bring me some gas . . . Hahaha! #pitstop #fuelmileage

RobbyGordon You really think I'd miss Sonoma?. . . . no way, car getting fixed and hope to test soon.

Regan_Smith: If anybody needs an electrician I think I might be the man for the job . . . been working on the RV since I got to Kansas, seems to have some pretty interesting electrical problems going on. If the lights go out around KC tonight, it's not my fault. Haha

2. Denny Hamlin tweets.

dennyhamlin (picture of Denny's car) If u see me today in ur rear view driving this . . Please move!!

dennyhamlin Just had to take my dog to a vet in dega . . I came back to my bus to find he ate all of my knee medication . . He's gonna be fine tho.

dennyhamlin Yea not good at all.. He also devoured an entire pair of sunglasses, ipad charger, the straps on my bookbag and 2 pillows . . #baddoggie

dennyhamlin I am now accepting all good luck charms. Tough ending yesterday but we will be back. SOON

dennyhamlin so my crew chief tells me all these different guys that will be on my radio this weekend in dega. i say good! now i won't have to flip them the bird. Now i can just tell them what i think . . .

1. Exchange Between Brett Griffin, Jimmie Johnson, DeLana Harvick, Kevin Harvick, and Michael Waltrip.

31n2Spotter (Brett Griffin): I'm sweatin like Denny Hamlin atta UPS store between Jimmie Johnson, Delana Harvick, Kevin Harvick and Michael Waltrip (who adds a picture)

JimmieJohnson Hey @KevinHarvick, can I have my horseshoe back? Please?

DeLanaHarvick oh come on, can't he keep it for just a little while longer? :) RT

DeLanaHarvick make a deal? he'll return it RT @jim_utter: @KevinHarvick won $406,786 for 600 win. Now I c y @JimmieJohnson wants his horseshoe bk

KevinHarvick I hope we can keep it a while!

mw55 (Michael Waltrip): Hey @Jimmie Johnson i found it! (picture of horseshoe) Not sure how we get it back up there.

Fans: Don't forget to send your tweets to twitter@racedayonspeed.

Imagine winning a NASCAR Sprint Cup Series race. Now, imagine getting on a serious roll and winning 10 in a row. Only the King has accomplished that feat (in 1967). He's also the only driver to have won six races in a row (in 1971). Bobby Allison won five races in a row that same year. To date, drivers have only won four in a row eight times in NASCAR's premier series. It gets a little bit easier for a driver to notch three in a row, with that happening 12 times.

Here are the three-peats and four-peats (listed chronologically) that drivers have pulled off in the modern era, along with the race tracks they accomplished them at.

Three in a Row

13. Bobby Allison (1972). Bristol, Trenton, Atlanta.

12. David Pearson (1973). Darlington, Martinsville, Talladega.

11. Richard Petty (1974). Atlanta, Pocono, Talladega.

10. Richard Petty (1975). Bristol, Atlanta, North Wilkesboro.

9. David Pearson (1976). Charlotte, Riverside, Michigan.

8. Bobby Allison (1983). Darlington, Richmond, Dover.

7. Dale Earnhardt Sr. (1987). Bristol, Darlington, Richmond.

6. Rusty Wallace (1988). Charlotte, North Wilkesboro, Rockingham.

5. Rusty Wallace (1993). Bristol, North Wilkesboro, Martinsville.

4. Rusty Wallace (1994). Dover, Pocono, Michigan.

3. Jeff Gordon (1996). Dover, Martinsville, North Wilkesboro.

2. Jeff Gordon (1998–1999). Rockingham, Atlanta, Daytona.

1. Jimmie Johnson (2004). Charlotte, Martinsville, Atlanta.

Four in a Row
8. Cale Yarborough (1976). Richmond, Dover, Martinsville, North Wilkesboro.

7. Darrell Waltrip (1981). Martinsville, North Wilkesboro, Charlotte, Rockingham.

6. Dale Earnhardt Sr. (1987). Darlington, North Wilkesboro, Bristol, Martinsville.

5. Harry Gant (1991). Darlington, Richmond, Dover, Martinsville.

4. Bill Elliott (1992). Rockingham, Richmond, Atlanta, Darlington.

3. Mark Martin (1993). Watkins Glen, Michigan, Bristol, Darlington.

2. Jeff Gordon (1998). Pocono, Indianapolis, Watkins Glen, Michigan.

1. Jimmie Johnson (2007). Martinsville, Atlanta, Texas, Phoenix.

Even though many won't admit it, most drivers have a favorite track. For certain drivers, there's just something about the twists and turns of a particular road course or the high-banked walls of a particular superspeedway that they not only like, but believe helps them perform there.

For Dale Earnhardt Jr., Talladega is his lucky charm; he is tied with Buddy Baker for most consecutive wins (four) at this track. Bill Elliott won four straight at Michigan, while the King and Darrell Waltrip are tied for the most consecutive wins (seven) at the same track (Petty at Richmond; Waltrip at Bristol).

Ten drivers in NASCAR history have won the same event at the same track at least four consecutive times. Here is a chronological rundown of those drivers, the events, and their (at minimum) four-time lucky tracks.

10. Dan Gurney. January Race at Riverside International Raceway (1963-66).

9. Richard Petty. Late July/Early August Race at Nashville Speedway (1964-67).

8. Richard Petty. Fall Race at Martinsville Speedway (1967-70).

7. Richard Petty. April Race at North Wilkesboro Speedway (1970-75).

6. Richard Petty. Fall Race at Richmond International Raceway (1970-74).

5. Darrell Waltrip. October Race at North Wilkesboro Speedway (1981-84).

4. Darrell Waltrip. Spring Race at Bristol Motor Speedway (1981-84).

3. Rusty Wallace. April Race at Martinsville Speedway (1993-96).

2. Jeff Gordon. Spring Race at Bristol Motor Speedway (1995-98).

1. Jeff Gordon. Fall Race at Darlington Raceway (1995-98).

When NASCAR was in its infancy, drivers drove the family car to the race track on a trailer. They worked on their cars in their own garage, and if they wrecked too badly on race day, they had to ask someone for a ride home.

From Ralph Earnhardt's garage in Kannapolis, North Carolina, to Dale Earnhardt's "Garage-Mahal," race shops have truly evolved. Today, they are not only technical wonders, but they have become NASCAR meccas, places that fans dream of visiting. Here are the most technologically advanced race shops in the business.

10. Wood Brothers Racing. In the early 1950s, the oldest continually operating—and one of the winningest—teams in NASCAR made its magic in Stuart, Virginia, first on Dobyns Road, then in a modern, expansive facility on Performance Drive. Today, the Wood Brothers, who are credited with inventing the modern pit stop and have scored wins in every decade for the last six decades, keep their shop in Harrisburg, North Carolina, near NASCAR's Charlotte hub. Trevor Bayne's win at the 2011 Daytona 500 has given the team a major boost.

9. Richard Petty Motorsports. The Concord, North Carolina–based facility houses the NASCAR Sprint Cup teams of AJ Allmendinger and Marcos Ambrose. The lobby is open to fans who sometimes get lucky enough to spot a man wearing a Charlie 1 Horse cowboy hat. Around this shop, the man is known simply as "R.P."

8. Earnhardt Ganassi Racing with Felix Sabates. When Earnhardt and Ganassi Racing with Felix Sabates merged in 2008, the team doubled its impressive history. As of 2009, the teams moved in together and currently share space in the uber impressive former CGRFS building.

Visitors are invited to check out a large pit box display, handle car parts and even to try on a HANS device.

7. Penske Racing. Sometimes referred to as the New York Yankees of racing, Penske Racing has 23 national championships (12 in IndyCar Series) to its credit. The setup at Penske's Mooresville, North Carolina, shop is befitting of one of motorsport's most elite organizations with a total of 70 NASCAR Sprint Cup Series wins (as of August 27, 2011) to its credit with drivers Rusty Wallace, Jeremy Mayfield, Ryan Newman, among others, including current drivers Kurt Busch and Brad Keselowski.

6. Stewart-Haas Racing. Fans visiting this vast facility in Kannapolis, North Carolina, are greeted by gigantic photos of youthful NASCAR Sprint Cup drivers Tony Stewart and Ryan Newman. Massive windows provide views of the activity on the race shop floor. Wear your sunglasses. This place epitomizes spit, polish and shine.

5. Michael Waltrip Racing. Raceworld, USA—the Cornelius, North Carolina, home of Michael Waltrip Racing—is an 11-acre complex where the team's race cars are built and fans have access to areas such as the machine shop, the gears and transmission area, and the fabrication department. What else can you say about a shop where the floor is polished several times a day by a small Zamboni?

4. Joe Gibbs Racing. In 1998, Joe Gibbs Racing broke ground for its new, 125,000-square-foot facility, which opened for business three years later. From the 35,000-square-foot fabrication area to the formidable engine-building area to the 100-seat auditorium, Gibbs' headquarters, which is equipped to handle five race teams, is beyond impressive.

3. Roush Fenway Racing. It's a flurry of activity at Roush's uber-impressive Concord, North Carolina, shop, where at any given time crew members are working furiously in the chassis fabrication shop or the sheet metal shop or wheeling a backup car into the paint booth, always with the goal of adding to the team's 124 wins as of August 27, 2011.

2. Richard Childress Racing. The "shop" is a sprawling campus that includes the RCR Racing Museum and a 47,000-square-foot fan paradise with 46 cars and one truck on display. If that's not enough, there is an area dedicated to wildlife and outdoor conservation featuring many of Childress's animal trophies from his many hunting adventures.

1. Hendrick Motorsports. The gleaming No. 88 and No. 48 cars on display in the lobby say it all. More than 550 engines are built or rebuilt every year at the bustling, 100-plus-acre Hendrick Motorsports complex. Some 500 people keep the place humming by continually working to add to its 197 wins as of August 27, 2011.

In the world of sports, race car drivers are among the most diminutive of athletes. At least that's the public perception. Compared to an NFL defensive lineman or an NBA power forward, these guys, with a few exceptions, are lean and mean.

But do drivers really have to be short or, shall we say, compact, to fit in a race car? Junior Johnson and Tiny Lund, not exactly small men, fit in stock cars and maneuvered them to the finish over and over.

In case you're curious, here's a sampling of how 25 NASCAR notables stack up. (Note: in some cases, we made our best educated guess due to conflicting sources).

25. Danica Patrick (5' 2"). When she came on the scene, some drivers said her size was an unfair advantage.

24. Jason Leffler (5' 3"). The "faux hawk" haircut may add an inch.

23. Rex White (5' 4"). Probably the smallest NASCAR Sprint Cup Series champion ever.

22. Joe Weatherly (5' 5"). One writer called him a "stubby leadfoot."

21. Bobby Hamilton Jr. (5' 5"). That's about right for a short-track owner.

20. Mark Martin (5' 6"). Race cars don't know how old you are or how tall you are.

19. Jeff Gordon (5' 7" or 5' 8"). Depending on which source you believe.

18. Tony Stewart (5' 9"). Packs a much taller punch.

17. Cale Yarborough (5' 9"). Not particularly short, but he looked small when he stood next to his buddy, Tiny Lund.

16. Kasey Kahne (5' 9"). The one-time midget-car series champ is taller than all that.

15. Kurt Busch (5' 11"). Just shy of six feet, but no one calls him shy.

14. Dale Earnhardt Jr. (6' 0"). Almost identical in height to his dad.

13. Denny Hamlin (6' 0"). Standing tall after 17 wins (and counting).

12. Kyle Busch (6' 1"). Eat your M&Ms and grow up tall.

11. Joey Logano (6' 1"). He's young. Is it possible he's not done growing?

10. Carl Edwards (6' 1"). Makes those backflips even more impressive.

9. Bill Elliott (6' 1"). Unassuming, but hard to miss at that height.

8. Richard Petty (6' 2"). Even taller with the hat.

7. Elliott Sadler (6' 2"). Fried bologna sandwiches are the secret to this guy's height.

6. Boris Said (6' 3"). Not including the hair.

5. Michael Waltrip (6' 4"). Looks down a bit on his brother Darrell, who stands 6' 1".

4. Bill France (6' 5"). An always-imposing presence.

3. Tiny Lund (6' 5"). A 300-pound-plus driving machine.

2. Buddy Baker (6' 6"). Most likely the tallest driver to ever race in NASCAR.

1. Brad Dougherty (7' 0"). The NBA star turned team owner and TV analyst is the tallest man in NASCAR. When he played for the Cleveland Cavaliers, he wore No. 43 in honor of Richard Petty.

There are plenty of times when drivers can't eat. The couple of hours it takes to run a 600-mile race come to mind, which made us wonder, while their cars are running and their stomachs are rumbling, do drivers fantasize about the perfect post-race meal? Here are driver's picks for their last meal:

16. Ricky Rudd: Fast food.

15. Dale Earnardt Jr.: Teriyaki steak.

14. Kyle Petty: Any type of seafood. Probably oysters or clams.

13. Mark Martin: Something healthy like orange roughy, a sweet potato, and grilled asparagus.

12. Aric Almirola: Steak from Charley's Steakhouse in Tampa. With a little sauce on it. And mint chocolate chip ice cream for dessert.

11. Kevin Harvick: Mexican food.

10. Kyle Busch: His mom's spaghetti.

9. Hermie Sadler: Steak and his mom's sweet potato casserole.

8. Matt Kenseth: His wife's chicken pot pie.

7. Kenny Wallace. Something from Cracker Barrel. Preferably pork chops, macaroni and cheese, corn bread, and sweet tea.

6. Elliott Sadler: As many Martinsville hot dogs as possible.

5. Jeff Gordon: Chipotle.

4. Tony Stewart: Whopper Jr. with cheese from Burger King, fries, and an ice cold Coca-Cola. And some Oreos.

3. Kurt Busch: A hot dog at Wrigley Field.

2. Jimmie Johnson: Mexican food. And ice cream.

1. Carl Edwards: Something that wouldn't make him look bloated in his coffin.

Best Intimidator Moments

Dale Earnhardt Sr., who was well-known as NASCAR's Intimidator, provided fans with countless special moments on the track and off the track. People are still talking about many of them, years after his death. Here are 10 that stand out to this day.

10. The Softer Side. Earnhardt's generosity is legendary in the NASCAR community. There are hundreds of stories of the Intimidator performing random acts of kindness for fans, fellow drivers, and just everyday folk. Often, his softer side came out when the cameras weren't rolling or reporters weren't around to record the event. But we know it was there.

9. Atlanta Motor Speedway (2000). Earnhardt's shootout with Bobby Labonte kept the fans on their feet.

8. Talladega Superspeedway (1984). Earnhardt's first win in his signature black No. 3 car.

7. Texas Motor Speedway (2000). Dale Earnhardt Jr. won the race in just his 12th NASCAR Sprint Cup Series race start. His dad, who showed up in Victory Lane with palpable fatherly pride, finished seventh.

6. Talladega Superspeedway (1996). Earnhardt had the points lead going into this race and was battling Sterling Marlin for the lead when Ernie Irvan, running third, tapped Marlin, who turned Earnhardt right into the wall. Despite the spectacular wreck, Earnhardt qualified the next week at the Brickyard, although Mike Skinner took over for him on race day.

5. Charlotte Motor Speedway (1987). As the 1987 NASCAR Sprint All-Star Race wound down, a nudge from Bill Elliott resulted in Earnhardt's famous "pass in the grass." Although it was technically more of a detour than a pass, Earnhardt's end run became one of the most famous moves in NASCAR history.

4. Indianapolis Motor Speedway (1995). The battle for the win at NASCAR's second-ever race at this storied track was between Rusty Wallace, Dale Jarrett, and Earnhardt. In the end, Earnhardt ran away with it.

3. Talladega Superspeedway (2000). No one knew it at the time, but the last-minute push from Kenny Wallace that put Dale Sr. over the top in this thrilling race would provide Earnhardt with what turned out to be his final NASCAR Sprint Cup win.

2. Bristol Motor Speedway (1998). Still working off the adrenaline of his Daytona 500 win, the Intimidator was on a roll that year and at Bristol he did it his way, spinning out Terry Labonte for the win. When asked about it afterwards, he famously said: "I didn't mean to wreck him. I just wanted to rattle his cage."

1. Daytona International Raceway (1998). Twentieth-time lucky. Earnhardt finally wins the Daytona 500.

Bibliography

nascar.com

speed.com

jayski.com

racing-reference.com

lvrj.com (*Las Vegas Review-Journal* website: Get to Know Your NASCAR Drivers, March 6, 2011).

si.com

espn.com

Drive Like Hell: NASCAR's Best Quotes and Quips, Eric Zweig (Firefly Books, 2007)

NASCAR: Races, Tracks and Superstars, Greg Fielden and the auto editors of *Consumer Guide* (Publications International, Ltd., 2007)

NASCAR and Racing Resources media guides (2011)

NASCAR: The Complete History, Greg Fielden with Bryan Hallman and the auto editors of *Consumer Guide*, (Publications International, Ltd., 2010)

NASCAR: Then and Now, Ben White (Motorbooks, 2010)

Official NASCAR Trivia: The Ultimate Challenge for NASCAR Fans (HarperCollins, 1998)

Speed, Guts, & Glory: 100 Unforgettable Moments in NASCAR History, Joe Garner (Warner Books, 2006)

The Wildest Ride: A History of NASCAR, Joe Menzer, (Simon & Schuster, 2001)

Forty Years of Stock Car Racing, Volumes 1- 4, and *Forty Plus Four, 1990-1993: First Supplement to the Forty Years of Stock Car Racing Series,* Greg Fielden (Galfield Press, 1994)

The Weekend Starts on Wednesday: True Stories of Remarkable NASCAR Fans, Andrew Giangola (Motorbooks, 2010)

Then Junior Said to Jeff: The Best NASCAR Stories Ever Told, David Poole and Jim McLaurin (Triumph Books, 2006)

The Ride of Their Lives (DVD), NASCAR Media Group, CMT Films 2009